Who the Hell is Jean Piaget?

Who the Hell is Jean Piaget?

And what are his theories all about?

Dr Jessica Koehler

BOWDEN
&BRAZIL

First published in Great Britain in 2021 by
Bowden & Brazil Ltd
Felixstowe, Suffolk, UK.

British Library Cataloguing-in-Publication Data
A CIP record for this book is available from The British Library.

Academic advisor: Jennifer Coe, University of Suffolk.

ISBN 978-1-8382286-5-1

To find out more about other books and authors in this series,
visit www.whothehellis.co.uk

Contents

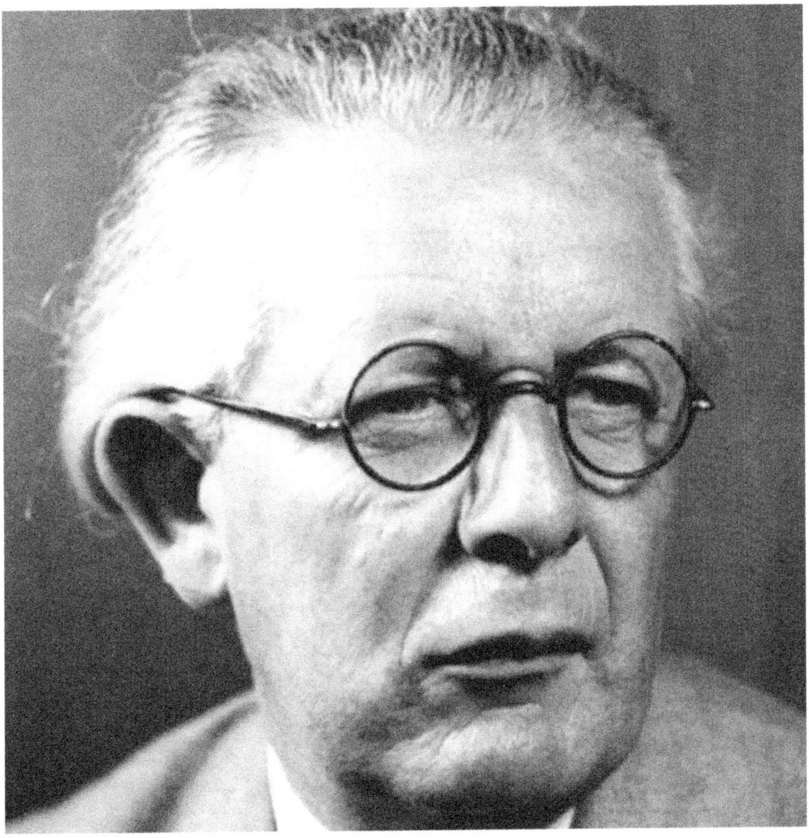

Introduction

Regarded as one of the most influential developmental psychologists of the 20th century, Jean Piaget was trained in the natural sciences, with his primary formal academic interest being biology. Later he became fascinated with children's intellectual development and his atypical educational background allowed him to perceive the progression of cognitive development in a novel way.

While his early years were filled with intensive studies of animal biology, Piaget's later curiosity about the unfolding progression of human knowledge acquisition and intelligence led to revolutionary ideas that forever changed the way we understand human development. Through his diverse educational experiences and relationships with other prominent psychologists, Piaget was able to perceive the developing child differently than his contemporaries. His deep understanding of cognitive development was further influenced by the time spent with his three children who became his primary research subjects.

Considered a developmental psychologist by most scholars, Piaget referred to himself as a genetic epistemologist. He was predominantly interested in the scientific understanding of how knowledge is acquired. This translated into decades of study to uncover how children acquire and construct knowledge. The constructivist approach defined Piaget's core belief about the progression of knowledge acquisition. To him, children actively construct their cognitions by being more than passive participants in their education. This view of knowledge acquisition was radical in the early 20th century and placed him at odds with contemporary theories about child development.

Throughout history, human behaviour has been conceptualized as stemming from nature or nurture. Proponents of the former believe that our underlying genetics are of primary importance in determining our developmental trajectory, while advocates of the latter regard cognitive development as primarily guided by environmental circumstances. Nature-oriented philosophers, such as Jean-Jacques Rousseau (1712–78), wrote about the naturally growing organism going through genetically pre-determined stages. For these thinkers, child development was guided by innate processes. On the other hand, philosopher John Locke (1632–1704) and psychologists John B. Watson (1878–1958) and B.F. Skinner (1904–90) viewed the mind as a machine of environmental inputs and behavioural outputs. For them the environment is fully responsible for human development. They considered genetic predeterminism as being of little significance and motivation for learning was seen as external.

Piaget, however, felt that cognitive development could not be accurately conceptualized by such a stark dichotomy. He held an interactionist viewpoint that suggested the child is a scientist, or explorer, constructing and organizing the world and their own development, meaning that the motivation for learning is internal rather than outside the individual.

Piaget's books and articles were originally written in French. The language and translation barrier, in addition to the behavioural zeitgeist that dominated American psychology, prevented his ideas from being widely studied and used in the United States until the 1960s. In addition, Piaget's highly academic writing style was challenging for many practitioners to understand. In the later years of Piaget's life much care was taken to work with prominent English-speaking psychologists to ensure that Piaget's ideas were accurately represented within the educational and psychological realms.

While the initial spread of Piaget's ideas was slow, eventually his notions about human knowledge acquisition proliferated throughout the fields of psychology and education. He is now one of the most widely cited authors within the field of child psychology, indicating the far-reaching influence of his groundbreaking ideas. His theories took time to resonate throughout the globe, but their widespread use across the world speaks volumes for the ingenuity and applicability of Piagetian concepts about cognitive development. Many schools and centres of education have organized themselves around Piaget's principles, which leaves his legacy moving far into the 21st century and beyond.

Who the Hell is Jean Piaget? begins with an overview of Piaget's life story before moving on to describe the numerous influences on Piaget's thinking that led to his groundbreaking ideas. We then look at three of his key ideas: his framework of genetic epistemology, which provides the foundation for all of his later ideas; his Stages of Cognitive Development; and an overview of his ideas on moral development. A final chapter details the ways in which Piaget's ideas have been applied to educational domains. This book sets out to provide the reader with a cohesive understanding of Jean Piaget's legacy and how he forever changed the fields of psychology and education.

1. Piaget's Life Story

Jean William Fritz Piaget was born on 9 August 1896 in Neuchâtel, Switzerland. He was the eldest child and only son of Arthur Piaget (1865–1952) and Rebecca-Suzanne Jackson (1872–1942) and had two younger sisters, Madeleine (1899–1976) and Marthe (1903–85). The Piaget family lived in the French-speaking region of Switzerland near Lake Neuchâtel, nestled in the Swiss Alps in an area known for its vineyards and watch- and clock-making. It was a canton (one of the states of the Swiss confederation) that quickly became a sanctuary for intellectuals, particularly those who were scientifically oriented, patriotic and had high religious morals. Towards the end of the 19th century through to the beginning of the 20th century, Neuchâtel grew considerably, largely due to industrialization. As a result, the canton was able to invest heavily in its educational system, building schools as well as two museums specializing in art and in natural history.

A Childhood of Critical Thinking vs. Religion

Piaget's father, Arthur, was from an old and wealthy family who had settled in Neuchâtel in the mid-17th century. Arthur was one of the leading figures in science and education in Neuchâtel

Fig. 1 Lake Neuchâtel, Switzerland, where Piaget grew up.

and was a highly successful professor of medieval literature and history at the university there, having studied for his degree in Paris and his PhD at the University of Geneva. It was while teaching in Paris at the Ecole Pratique des Hautes Etudes that he had met Jean's mother, Rebecca, who was working as a primary school teacher. Rebecca's family were English immigrants who had made their money through English steel and whose elevated position in Parisian society gave Arthur an entry into the Protestant upper class of the capital.

Jean's early childhood was influenced greatly by witnessing his father's intense academic drive and high morals. He regarded Arthur as 'a man of a painstaking and critical mind, who dislikes hastily improvised generalizations, and is not afraid of starting a fight when he finds historic truth twisted to fit respectable traditions' (Piaget quoted in Kohler, 2008). Over the course of his academic career, Arthur had caused several ripples in the conservative canton which were deemed unpatriotic by revealing the truth behind several local historical myths. Despite avoiding any repercussions in terms of promotion (he was appointed manager of the state historical archives, in the face of much opposition; headed up the editorial office of the *Neuchâtel Museum* journal, and was appointed founding rector at the university), Arthur was excluded from the aristocratic traditionalists who were dominant in the canton.

Nonetheless, Arthur's reputation as a philologist of world renown remained strong and he was highly respected by his colleagues and students alike at the university. His position at the university meant that Jean was drawn into the world of academia from an early age, with his father actively encouraging his natural curiosity about the world. Arthur taught Jean the importance of systematic work and the ethics of achievement, and his extensive connections gave Jean access to many academic societies and publishers.

Jean's mother, Rebecca, gave up work as a teacher when she married and she settled to life as a mother and homemaker. Jean described his mother as 'very intelligent, energetic, and fundamentally a very kind person' (Piaget quoted in Kohler, 2008). However, she was also reportedly an emotionally unbalanced woman and, although Jean was very fond of her, he was also often unnerved by her due to the relative dysfunction she created within the family. It has been suggested that Rebecca's mental illness was the reason for Piaget spending part of his childhood in Paris with his grandmother.

Rebecca was a devout Protestant and brought her children up to follow her faith, sending Jean to Sunday school from age 7 to 12 which was followed by youth service, and then religious instruction from age 14 to 16. Being an intelligent child, Jean would begin to question religious dogma as he got older which would initiate a life-long search for a way to reconcile his faith in God with the reality of the world. While preparing for his confirmation, Piaget remembers:

> *'Two things struck me at the time: on the one hand the difficulty of reconciling a number of dogmas with biology, and on the other, the fragility of the "five" proofs of the existence of God [...] Though I would not even have dreamed of denying the existence of God, the fact that anyone should reason by such weak arguments [...] seemed to me all the more extraordinary since my pastor was an intelligent man, who himself dabbled in the natural sciences!'* (Piaget, 1952)

This querying of dogmas reflects the contrasting minds of his parents: that of his critically thinking father and that of his devoutly religious mother.

Rebecca was also politically motivated, joining her husband in the cause of separation between Church and State in 1907, and becoming the first socialist to be elected to the local school commission in 1912, whereby she had a voice in how the school was managed and controlled. She was also an active pacifist, writing a report on a refugee camp near Lake Geneva, which was published in the local newspaper. In the report, Rebecca accused the Germans of being 'invaders' and 'barbarians'. Witnessing his mother's altruistic behaviour alongside her mental health problems, likely contributed to Piaget's interest in psychoanalysis and psychopathology as a way for him to cope and understand the conflicting feelings towards his mother that he must surely have felt.

A Child Prodigy

As an adult, Piaget described his childhood as being somewhat difficult and it is perhaps for this reason that he immersed himself in his studies. He was a serious child, driven by his pursuit of knowledge and – being somewhat of a child prodigy – he achieved top grades in all his classes throughout his time at school. However, he became easily bored in class, finding the routines and regimented curriculum stifling. He gained access to the library at the university and devoured books and journals there in his bid to solve the mysteries of nature.

At an early age, Jean exhibited advanced interest in the natural world, emulating his father's passionate curiosity and desire to learn. Jean was initially fascinated by zoology, finding the behaviour, classification, and physiology of animals in his surrounding Swiss environment captivating. Oftentimes, he could be found studying the biology of mollusks (an extensive phylum of invertebrates that includes slugs, snails, squid, mussels, and clams) in nearby watering holes – a passion that ignited his interest in understanding the development of a variety of organisms.

Malacology at the Museum

In 1907, at the age of 10, Jean wrote a report on his observations of a partly albino sparrow he observed in a park and sent it to *Le Rameau de Sapin* (The Fir Branch) which was the associated journal of the natural-science youth club. Much to Jean's delight and pride, it was published which prompted him to write to the director of the Museum of Natural History, Paul Godet (1836–1911), who was also a biology teacher and a friend of Jean's father, to ask if he might be allowed to study the collections of

Fig. 2 Museum of Natural History, Neuchâtel, Switzerland.

fossils, shells and birds at the museum in his spare time. Godet agreed and invited Jean to assist him at the museum twice a week. Godet's work included compiling a large collection of mollusks in order to complete his taxonomy for a mollusk catalogue of Switzerland. Jean was given the task of searching for mollusks, which he duly did over the course of the next seven years, receiving some rare specimens for his own collection at home as payment. By all accounts, Godet was fond of the young Jean and provided him with the affection that was perhaps missing at home.

In 1910, Jean joined the Friends of Nature Club, which was to provide him with plenty of social and intellectual stimulus that would stand him in good stead for a career in science. Club activities included debates and presentations at which Jean became very adept. Upon the death of Godet the following year, part of his mollusk collection was donated to the club, along with books and equipment. Jean took it upon himself to carry on with Godet's work of finding and classifying specimens and, with thc help of Otto Fuhrmann (1871–1945) who took over the Chair of Zoology from Godet, Jean's scientific career began before he had even finished high school. Fuhrmann put Jean in touch with specialists and, with his encouragement, Jean began to write and publish articles. Fuhrmann sent one of Jean's articles to Maurice Bedot (1859–1927), professor and director of the Natural Science Museum of Geneva. Bedot, not realizing that the article had in fact been written by a schoolboy, offered Jean an assistants position. Jean replied, in a letter dated 10 May 1912: 'The position of assistant in malacology you are so kind to mention would please me very much, but I cannot consider it before the end of my high school studies, that is, three years from now.' (Kohler, 2008)

Piaget kept up correspondence with Bedot over the years and even worked at the museum of Geneva. His relationship with both Fuhrmann and Bedot as well as other academics they introduced him to helped him enormously and he went on to publish more than 20 articles on malacology (the study of mollusks) in scientific journals before he had even left school.

Introducing Philosophy

In the summer of 1912, Jean was invited to go to Annecy to stay with his godfather, Samuel Cornut (1861–1918). Cornut, a noted Swiss intellectual, felt that Jean's interest in malacology was too specialized and intended to steer his young godson's intellectually curious mind towards a deeper understanding of philosophy. Thus, Jean became interested in the philosophy of the French writer Henri Bergson (1859–1941). Bergson's 1907 book, *Creative Evolution* suggests that evolution is motivated by humanity's creative impulses. His belief in the theory of knowledge and the theory of life being inseparable was to guide Piaget for decades as he uncovered the way children learn and build knowledge. We will look at this in more detail in Chapter 2.

By 1913, Piaget was discussing Bergson's ideas enthusiastically with his peers at the Friends of Nature Club, resulting in many a heated debate. Jean's introduction to the world of Bergson and philosophy by his godfather would lead him to question the concept of God further: 'Instead of finding science's last word therein, as my godfather had let me hope, I got the impression of an ingenious construction without an experimental basis.' (Piaget, 1952)

An intelligent child, Jean sought out various philosophies in a bid to understand the inconsistencies he observed between what he was taught by the church and what he knew to be true of the natural world. As a result, his religiosity evolved from an emphasis on the organized, traditional religion by his mother towards a focus on a more personal and less structured relationship with God (Piaget, 1952).

Piaget at University

Graduating from Neuchâtel Latin High School, Jean went to the University of Neuchâtel, where his father had been rector (head of the university) up until 1911, to study natural sciences. From 1913 to 1915, Jean attended the lectures of Arnold Reymond (1874–1958) on psychology, logic and epistemology, and the history of philosophy. Reymond taught Piaget that logic and mathematics could be applied to the processes of life which would later influence him in his experiments in the cognitive development of children (see Chapter 4).

Fig. 3 University of Neuchâtel, Switzerland.

While at university, Piaget published several papers and was soon widely regarded as an expert in the study of mollusks. Zoologists around Switzerland came to regard the teenage Piaget as a knowledgeable authority. He was fascinated by the development of mollusks that he observed in nearby lakes in Switzerland. Specifically, he was interested in how mollusks were able to adapt from being transferred from one environment to another – a prelude to his life-long obsession with understanding the contributions of nature (underlying biological influence) versus nurture (underlying environmental influence) in the developing human.

Piaget noted that the shell structures of mollusks would physically adapt to rough or calm water; this was a groundbreaking discovery for the time. His observations and resulting research indicated that development was a process of complex interaction between an individual organism and its surrounding environment.

Shortly after taking his Baccalaureate exams – in which he achieved top grades – Piaget became ill and was forced to take a year off in the mountains to recover. He went to a health resort in Leysin at the eastern end of Lake Geneva from September 1915 to April 1916, then again in July that same year until the following February, 1917, and a final visit in the summer. He was treated by Dr Louis Vauthier, who later married Piaget's sister, Madeleine. In Richard Kohler's study of Piaget (2008), it is suggested that Piaget's stay in the mountains was for psychological reasons, rather than medical ones. Whatever the reason, a rest period in the mountains became a habitual trip which would continue for the rest of Piaget's life. His relationship with the natural world was something that he viewed as absolutely necessary to live a balanced life.

Time spent in the mountains certainly seemed to ignite Jean's creativity: by the age of 21, his collection of professionally published papers was remarkable. Twenty-five papers at such a young age was – and still is – viewed as an incredible accomplishment by a scholar in any field. He was one of the few experts in the study of mollusks, which made him a target for academic opportunities around Europe. In 1918, Piaget received his PhD from the University of Neuchâtel. His major area of study was natural science and he continued to build a reputation as an erudite scholar within the fields of biology and zoology at a surprisingly young age. His work in the biological fields propelled him to believe that human development was due to a combination of genetics (maturation) combined with environmental variables.

Becoming Piaget: The Scholar

Piaget's academic evolution of study proceeded from biology to philosophy to psychology. Two formal essays reveal this transition. In his paper, 'Biology and War' (1918), Piaget examines the ideas of Charles Darwin (1809–82) and Jean Baptist Lamarck (1744–1829). While Piaget concurs with the environmental and biological interactionism viewpoints regarding the development of human beings, he rejects the belief that war is a natural outcome of being human. Rather, his viewpoint is remarkably more positive suggesting that as humans develop, rather than becoming more aggressive, the effort to understand ourselves will move us further from inevitable paths of war and closer to an altruistic society.

The second marker of his evolution of thought came with his autobiographical novel *Recherche* (1918). As we have already noted, Piaget had often struggled to make sense of the intersection of religion and science. He was foremost a scientist – evaluating life through the lends of empiricism. However, he was also a religious man deeply connected to a more spiritual understanding of the world, and his mother's strict Calvinism lurked within him. *Recherche* became the stimulus for Piaget's ability to come to terms with the dichotomy of science and religion. Within it, he resolves his crisis by recognizing that while science generates laws, it is faith that acts as the motive force. The novelization of this crisis was described eloquently by Gruber and Voneche (1977):

> *'Then the "blinding discovery": science gives knowledge of good and of evil. It can explain everything, but it*

> *says nothing about values. It is faith that speaks to them. Faith is not knowledge, it is action. The contradiction between faith and knowledge is thus resolved. The final phase of the search is reconstruction; science gives laws of the world; faith is its engine.'*

So, just prior to embarking on his decades-long search to comprehend cognitive development, Piaget determined that there is a place for knowledge and science (intelligence) and a place for values and affectivity (faith). This important resolution allowed him to move past a potential looming intellectual crisis that could have side-tracked his professional career and altered his path to becoming one of the most prominent thinkers of the 20th century.

In 1918, following the completion of his doctoral degree in the natural sciences at the young age of 22, Piaget shifted his professional focus to the field of psychology. This new professional path was born out of the union of his interests in biology and philosophy. While both fields had captivated his attention, he knew he needed to apply the scientific methodologies of a biologist to the study of the developing mind. He had become frustrated with his short foray into philosophy; desiring more verifiable solutions, he knew he wanted to work with an experimental focus:

> *'The first reason for my growing disaffection with the traditional methods of philosophy was caused in the main by the conflict, which I felt within myself, between the habits of verification of the biologist and the psychologist, and speculative reflection, which constantly*

tempted me, but which could not possibly be submitted to verification...' (Piaget, 1972)

From Zurich to Paris to Geneva

In the autumn of 1918, Piaget enrolled at the University of Zurich for postdoctoral study where he immersed himself in psychological experimentation. Initially he was disappointed by the lectures that he attended on philosophy, mental development and pedagogy as they 'seemed to me to have little bearing on fundamental problems' (Piaget, 1952). Being a Protestant establishment, the University of Zurich welcomed religious and moral issues and Piaget had been hoping to study the origin of religious manifestations in the unconscious. He became captivated by psychoanalysis under the tutelage of eminent Swiss psychiatrist, Dr. Carl Jung (1875–1961) whose lectures he attended. Piaget was especially interested in Jung's emphasis on increasing a patient's consciousness to achieve balance and wholeness and on the importance of establishing a relationship between ego and self. As Piaget began to focus on understanding the processes of psychological experimentation, he moved away from studying biological processes. He worked in the famous psychiatric clinic of Dr. Eugen Bleuler (1857–1939) where he was introduced to the works of Sigmund Freud (1856–1939). Piaget

Fig. 4 Dr. Eugen Bleuler (1857–1939)

rejected Freudian psychoanalysis, however, due to its irrational, non-scientific approach to understanding human behaviour.

At this time, Piaget studied psychology only in French and therefore wasn't aware of psychological theories in other languages, namely the Gestalt psychologists Max Wertheimer (1880–1943) and Wolfgang Kohler (1887–1967). In an interview Piaget claimed that, had he studied Gestalt psychology when he was 18, he may well have become a Gestalt psychologist (Gale, 2015). Like the Gestalt psychologists, Piaget was interested in understanding cognition from a holistic perspective – with its emphasis on mental structures and an overall push towards equilibrium within the individual.

Piaget left his studies in Zurich after just one semester and moved to Paris. He explains:

> *'In the spring of 1919 I became restless and left for le Valais; there I applied Lipp's statistical method to a biometric study of the variability of land mollusks as a function of altitude! I needed to get back to concrete problems to avoid grave errors.'* (Piaget, 1952)

Piaget studied psychology, psychopathology, logic, and scientific philosophy at the Sorbonne for two years starting after the summer of 1919. This was to be an important time for Piaget. Lectures that Piaget attended included those of the philosopher and physician Pierre Janet (1859–1947) who taught experimental and comparative psychology and who was lecturing on the evolution of the personality for the time that Piaget was attending. Another part of Piaget's studies took the form of a practical tutorial with Théodore Simon (1873–1961) who taught experimental pedagogy and supervised intelligence research. This tutorial would lead to Simon mentoring Piaget and offering him a research post at the Alfred Binet laboratory. Simon was a prominent researcher who is credited alongside Alfred Binet (1857–1911) with developing the first-ever formal intelligence test – the Simon-Binet Test.

In December 1919, Piaget gave a presentation which showed just how much he had absorbed of his studies. He had discovered that, by applying psychoanalysis to pedagogy, the main educational problem was that of adults blaming children:

> '*With children, transfer lies at the base of all their feelings. Transfer explains the most banal actions. Thus a teacher often becomes a father symbol and the pupil uses him as a target for all his unsatisfied desires to revolt. Being thus aware and combining it with our knowledge regarding the development of complexes this must in turn transform pedagogy. It will no longer be a matter of punishing but of understanding.*' (Piaget quoted in Kohler, 2008)

The fundamental basis of Piaget's pedagogic theory was thus established when he was only 23 years old.

Piaget began conducting experimental studies with students at the École de la rue de la Grange-aux-Belles, a boys'

Fig. 5 Alfred Binet (1857–1911)

school next door to Binet's laboratory. It was here that he had his eureka moment on the genesis of knowledge within the human mind. We will look at this in more detail in Chapter 2. Piaget stayed at Binet's lab school for two years, perfecting his methodology and then, in 1921, he wrote a paper on his study and sent it to Edouard Claparède (1873–1940) who was the founder of the Jean-Jacques Rousseau Institute in Geneva, Switzerland, and also the editor of the journal *Archives de Psychologie*. In the paper he writes that logic is not an inherent attribute but instead develops over time through an adaptive process that is universal to everyone. Claparède accepted Piaget's paper and, through Piaget's mentor Pierre Bovet (1878–1965), who was Director of the Institute, he was offered the position of research psychologist. The Rousseau Institute was renowned for its educational research programs and was responsible for validating and publicizing the ideas of the New Education (a movement that promoted pedagogy as a way to achieve social advancement).

Fig. 6 Piaget with Pierre Bovet (front row) in front of the Rousseau Institute, Geneva, 1925.

Piaget transferred his program of study in Paris to his new academic position in Geneva. His paper was acknowledged as his 'habilitation' (the qualification he needed to obtain his PhD) and, after formalizing his field of study which would primarily focus on investigating the cognitive development of children, Piaget became a private lecturer at 25 years old.

Piaget the Husband, Father and Man

While working at the Rousseau Institute, Piaget fell in love with one of his colleagues, Valentine Châtenay (1899–1983), who had also studied psychology at the Institute. A few years later in 1923, they married and Valentine became Jean's research associate and a wonderful intellectual companion working side-by-side with Piaget on many of his academic pursuits. Piaget and Valentine went on to have three children, Jacqueline in 1925, Lucienne in 1927, and Laurent in 1931, who Jean and Valentine studied in-depth from infancy onward. In fact, their children were the primary research subjects throughout Piaget's long research career, which was and is an unusual approach in a scientific field. Together, Jean and Valentine became enthralled with watching their children's knowledge acquisition and their unfolding development. Their distinctive vantage point contributed to a unique understanding of the intricacies of human development. By observing his children, Piaget became an ethologist of human beings, interested in the genesis of knowledge and morality within humans.

However, Piaget was keen to point out that his children 'received an excellent education, thanks to the fact that I did not concern myself with their education at all. My wife was in charge of the children's education. I mainly observed them' (Piaget quoted in Kohler, 2008). While a loving father, who spent time with his children at the dinner table, at weekends and on holidays, there was a strict rule that he was not to be disturbed when he was working. Piaget's relationship with his children wasn't unlike the relationship he had with his own father. It was on more of an intellectual level, with his son saying that, at times, he felt 'a little intimidated' (Kohler, 2008).

By all accounts Piaget was a big man – well over six feet tall, broad and strong looking. He wore his hair long and had a wardrobe of almost identical suits. According to Dr Joan Bliss, who studied child development with Piaget at the University of Geneva, in the winter Piaget would wear a grey woollen cardigan over his waistcoat because he felt the cold and outdoors he would often add a beret, worn at a jaunty angle (Bliss, 2010). Bliss describes Piaget as a somewhat eccentric character with a great sense of humour. 'He invariably wore hobnailed walking boots rather than shoes, whatever the occasion' and had a 'meerschaum pipe, held more or less permanently between his teeth'. Bliss recounts how 'in his waistcoat pockets there permanently resided a miniature silver-handled knife used to peel and cut cloves of garlic, which he added to nearly every meal' as well as 'a large fob watch on a chain' which he 'used to time every event in which he was involved'. When travelling he would wrap all his research reports into a blanket which he tied 'to the end of a pole swung over his shoulder'. He was known for cycling around Geneva on a very old bicycle, on which he was filmed taking part 'in the tail end of the Tour de France, as it swung by him on his regular route alongside Lac Léman' (Bliss, 2010).

Fig. 7 Piaget with his wife Valentine (top right) at a conference at the International Bureau of Education in Geneva in 1932.

Finding Fame

In 1925, the same year that his first child Jacqueline was born, Piaget returned home to take up a position at Neuchâtel University as Professor of Philosophy and Psychology. His reputation was beginning to grow and in 1928 he met Albert Einstein who prompted Piaget to begin studying a child's conception of time, focusing on notions of simultaneity. Piaget was quite in awe of the great physicist, remarking that he 'impressed me profoundly, because he took an interest in everything' (Gale, 2015).

By the age of 30, Piaget was already a famous psychologist. His tireless work ethic and his prolific writings – dozens of books and hundreds of journal articles – propelled his everlasting influence in the fields of psychology and education. While Piaget was a workhorse, he was always collegial and kind, crediting many of his colleagues for their help with his unimaginable productivity. Of interest to many, who later tried to comprehend his large academic output, was his yearly ventures away from civilization.

Each summer, when the academic year ended, Piaget would collect his research findings and escape to an old farmhouse in the Alps alone. He spent time in isolation—away from family and friends, walking and exploring nature. This mental recharge appeared to be when Piaget was able to mentally rejuvenate and conceptualize his groundbreaking ideas as he would return from the mountains with one or two new books and several academic articles. He had learned early on his life, after his illness at university, that solitary time spent in nature recharged his body and mind and allowed him to be incredibly creative and productive.

In 1929, Piaget was offered a position back in Geneva teaching the history of scientific thought at the university. It would appear that he was somewhat relieved to be able to concentrate on psychology and sociology again, now that he had been 'freed from the hold of philosophy' (Piaget quoted in Kohler, 2008). At the same time, he was appointed Director of the International Bureau of Education (IBE) and Deputy Director of the Jean-Jacques Rousseau Institute (JJRI). Over the following 10 years, alongside his associates, he researched the development of logical thinking in children aged from 4 to 12, concentrating on concepts of movement, speed, time, space, number, quantity and geometry. It was at the University of Geneva that Piaget met Professor Bärbel Inhelder (1913–1997), who was an experimental psychologist there, and with who he collaborated on several publications and research projects on child development over the next 40 years. In a field dominated by men, Piaget was effective in bringing the work of female psychologists to the forefront; another psychologist that he collaborated and co-wrote books with being Alina Szeminska (1908–1986).

World War II

As the rumblings of WWII began, Piaget clung to his faith that all would be well: 'With the war looming, our civilization has reached a more critical point than ever before [...] I am more convinced than ever that education is the only remedy against evil.' (Piaget quoted in Kohler, 2008). However, as some of his colleagues were arrested in Germany's bid to 'cleanse' educational institutions of Jews and left-wing intellectuals, Piaget's hope for an education that was 'capable of saving our society from its potential violent or gradual dissolution' began to fade. He concludes that 'the teaching of international co-operation [...] was exceedingly superficial and avoided the real psychological motives for action' (Piaget quoted in Kohler, 2008). As a consequence, Piaget took the step of changing the public appearance of both the IBE and the JJRI, so that they were no longer seen to be an agency of the New Education movement, but instead simply neutral unbiased educational establishments.

Piaget played the political game carefully throughout the war, concentrating on his work and continuing to give lectures. In 1942, he held a series of lectures at the Collége de France in occupied Paris, which he voiced as an act of solidarity with his friends (years later, his lectures would be compiled into a book, The Psychology of Intelligence, which was published in 1963). Back in Switzerland, a month after the Americans had entered the war, Piaget gave a lecture at the Elementary School Teachers' Congress in Bern. The lecture was on 'Education Towards Freedom' and he argued for freedom of thought and morality and freedom of political views. However, he didn't cross the line in criticizing totalitarian regimes.

Piaget's Factory

From the end of WWII, Piaget set his sights on completing his bold project of coming up with a scientific theory for the origins of knowledge. In 1950, he published his major work *Introduction à l'épistémologie génétique* in three volumes. It wasn't until after 1950 that Piaget's work began to become known outside of Europe. In 1955, through a grant from the Rockefeller Foundation, Piaget established the International Centre for Genetic Epistemology (ICGE) in Geneva. At this time, Piaget was a faculty member at the University of Geneva. His newly developed centre focused on studying the unfolding acquisition of knowledge and quickly became known as 'Piaget's factory'. Each year, eminent scholars from varied fields visited the centre and conducted research in many disparate domains of study. Because Piaget believed knowledge was best pursued from an interdisciplinary perspective, the centre had scholars from the fields of physics, biology, mathematics, language, psychology, and education.

In 1968, during the student uprisings, Piaget was the target of severe criticism by both striking students and professors at the University of Geneva. It seems that they were unhappy with the power he held over 80 assistants and 400 students in his capacity as chair of the department. While he garnered support from many of his colleagues, he lost some of his assistants. A few years later in 1971, he resigned after 50 years of teaching and his chair was divided between his colleagues. Jacques Vonèche took over child and adolescent psychology while Bärbel Inhelder replaced him in genetic epistemology and experimental psychology.

Over the next decade, despite his official retirement, Piaget continued as director of the ICGE where he carried out further research on causality, necessity, possibility and logic. In 1976, at the age of 80, Piaget humorously decided it was about time to present himself for a colloquium (whereby a PhD candidate presents a paper in order to receive their qualification) as he had never officially obtained an academic qualification to teach epistemology, psychology and sociology. He spoke in front of a jury on his latest work *The Development of Thought: Equilibration of Cognitive Structures* (1975). However, as the university couldn't officially recognize this examination, Piaget declared 'I shall die without an actual degree [in psychology] and shall take the secret of my educational shortcomings to my grave' (Piaget quoted in Kohler, 2008). Piaget directed the centre until his death in 1980.

Piaget's Death and Legacy

As Piaget became an octogenarian, his health began to go downhill. Having always been a pipe smoker, his smoking finally began to take its toll. According to his colleague at the university, Dr Jean Bliss (2010), 'When his doctor told him to reduce his smoking he simply halved the amount of tobacco in each fill of his pipe, converting four pipe-fulls into eight half pipe-fulls a day'. Alas In 1979, he developed an abscess in his lungs and became seriously ill. After a spell in hospital he managed to attend the XXV symposium of the ICGE, held in June 1980. Three months later on 16 September, Piaget was taken to hospital in Geneva where he died at the age of 84. He was buried at the *Cimètiere des Plainpalais* in Geneva alongside his wife, Valentine; a place of rest where other eminent names such as John Calvin, Jorge Luis Borges, and Ernest Ansermet are buried.

Throughout his long career, Piaget wrote many books and papers, edited numerous scientific journals and received over 30 honorary degrees from some of the most prestigious universities. He became the first European cited by the American Psychological Association (APA) for his distinguished contribution to the field of psychology. This award elucidates the groundbreaking contributions that Piaget made to the field of psychology on a world-wide scale and led to him often being labelled one of the most important intellectuals of the 20th century. By many accounts, he was certainly one of the most productive academics of that time period. According to the APA, Piaget was able to bridge the gulf between the worlds of philosophy and biological science by utilizing new methodologies to understand the evolution of human knowledge acquisition. The citation from the APA at the time of his award (1969) was a clear indication of Piaget's pioneering ideas: 'He has approached questions up to now exclusively philosophical in a resolutely empirical manner, and has made epistemology into a science separate from philosophy, but related to all the human sciences.' (APA, 1969). Since his death, Piaget's ideas have been widely translated and spread around the world. Their influence on child psychology and education is immeasurable and continues into the 21st century.

Fig. 8 Bust of Jean Piaget in Parc des Bastion in Geneva, Switzerland.

Jean Piaget's Timeline

Jean Piaget

- **1896** Jean Piaget is born
- **1899** Piaget's sister Madeleine is born
- **1903** Piaget's youngest sister, Marthe, is born
- **1907** Begins working with Paul Godet at the Museum of Natural History
- **1912** Offered position at the Natural Science Museum of Geneva, but is too young to accept.
- **1915** Receives Baccalaureate degree from the University of Neuchâtel
- **1918** Obtains PhD in Natural Science from the University of Neuchâtel; enrols at University of Zurich for postdoctoral study
- **1919** Begins two years of studying at the Sorbonne in Paris
- **1920** Research at Alfred Binet's Laboratory
- **1921** First article published on psychology of intelligence; offered position at the Rousseau Institute in Geneva
- **1923** First of nearly 60 books published; Marries Valentine Châtenay
- **1925** Piaget's first child, Jacqueline, is born; Returns to Neuchâtel University as Professor of Philosophy and Psychology
- **1927** Piaget's second child, Lucienne, is born
- **1929** Appointed Director of International Bureau of Education and Deputy Director of Rousseau Institute
- **1931** Piaget's third child, Laurent, is born

World Events

- **1896** First modern Olympic games held in Athens, Greece
- **1900** British Labour Party is officially established
- **1906** San Francisco Earthquake
- **1914** Outbreak of World War I
- **1918** End of World War I
- **1919** Prohibition begins in the United States
- **1918-20** Spanish Flu
- **1922** Irish Free State gains independence from United Kingdom
- **1923** Mount Etna erupts in Italy
- **1927** Pavlov publishes *Conditioned Reflexes*
- **1928** Watson and Rayner publish *The Psychological Care of Infant and Child*
- **1929** Beginning of the Great Depression

1936 Receives honorary doctorate from Harvard University, USA

1940 Becomes President of the Swiss Society of Psychology

1942 Piaget's mother dies

1945 Named President of the Swiss Commission of UNESCO

1946 Receives honorary doctorate from the Sorbonne, Paris

1950 Publishes major work, ***Introduction à l'èpistemologie génétique***

1952 Becomes professor at the Sorbonne; Piaget's father dies

1955 Establishes the International Centre for Genetic Epistemology in Geneva, known as 'Piaget's Factory'

1969 American Psychological Association Award for Distinguished Scientific Contributions to Psychology

1971 Resigns from University of Geneva after 50 years of teaching

1976 Daughter, Madeleine, dies

1980 Jean Piaget dies in Geneva, Switzerland

1934 Lev Vygotsky dies

1936 Ivan Pavlov dies

1939 World War II begins; Sigmund Freud dies

1941 Japanese attack on Pearl Harbor

1945 World War II ends

1947 Cold War begins; The sound barrier is broken for the first time

1952 The Great Smog of London descends, killing over 10,000 people

1953 Crick and Watson discover the helical structure of DNA

1955 US involvement in the Vietnam War begins

1961 Theodore Simon dies

1962 Cuban Missile Crisis

1968 Student and worker uprisings in France

1969 Stonewall riots in New York City, USA

1971 B.F. Skinner featured on the cover of *Time* magazine

1980 Mt St. Helens erupts in Washington, USA; The Rubik's Cube and Pacman make their debut to the world

2. Influences on Piaget's Thinking

The influences on Piaget were many and varied. From early childhood, Piaget's interest in biology, due in part to his location in Switzerland, opened his eyes to the possibilities waiting for him in the study of zoology and evolution. From there, he briefly became enthralled with philosophy, but quickly realized that his earlier scientific experimentation commanded a more scientific framework for understanding the world. Experiences following his doctoral program led him into psychology and specifically into his lifelong quest to uncover the origins of human knowledge acquisition.

A Foundation in Biology

Piaget's time spent at the Neuchâtel Museum of Natural History under the tutelage of Paul Godet meant that he was immersed in science from early childhood. Helping Godet to collect mollusks for classification and later taking over his mentor's life's project led to Piaget not only adopting Godet's field of research but also his scientific viewpoint. Godet followed the Lamarckist understanding of evolution whereby an organism can pass on physical characteristics to its offspring that it has acquired through use or disuse during its lifetime. Godet believed that it

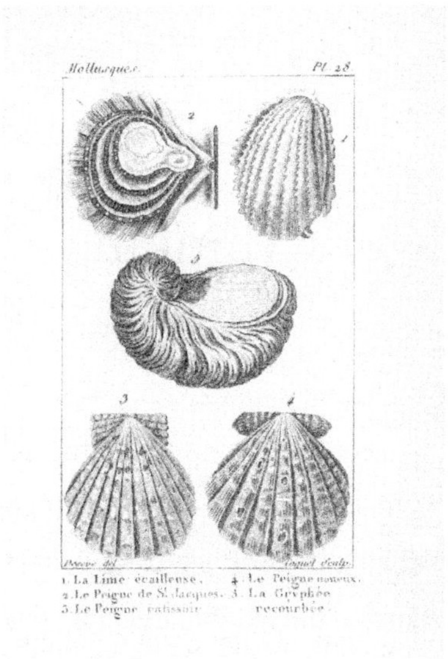

Fig. 9 An example of the taxonomy of mollusks, 1843.

was more important to correctly classify phenomena than to verify hypotheses through experiments. Thereby he was most interested in scaling down the number of species by classifying them as varieties of a higher species. He taught the young Piaget the complex rules of terminology when classifying mollusks and when Piaget took over the project he commemorated his teacher by naming a variety after him.

There can be little doubt that Godet played a large part in Piaget's intellectual development. When Piaget took up the professorship at Neuchâtel University in 1925, he continued his research on mollusks and, using biometrics (detecting and recording physical traits), he studied the influence that an organism's actions would have on the hereditary character. Alongside his lab work, he observed the habit-forming behaviour and reflexes of his newborn daughter, Jacqueline. For Piaget psychology was a biological science and he was determined to find a new theory of evolution.

Philosophical Beginnings

The time that Piaget spent with his godfather Samuel Cornut provided him with stimulation, allowing him to take a deep dive into the fields of philosophy and epistemology, which may have been one of the sparks that moved him towards his later research specializations. Cornut's influence likely pushed Piaget to look beyond his vast knowledge of the biological sciences to an interdisciplinary view that encompassed philosophy, logic, and religion to supplement his formal education. Even from an early age, as an aspiring biologist, Piaget was seeking to understand an explanation of knowledge development (Wadsworth, 2004). While biology was his first intellectual love, it was this meshing of biological and philosophical questions that led to his later career trajectory. The quest to uncover the origins of knowledge and cognitive maturity stayed with him throughout his long and celebrated career.

Bergson's *Élan Vital*

The philosopher that made the most marked impression on Piaget was Henri Bergson. His theory of the *élan vital* (vital force) directed Piaget's interest in evolution to the areas of adaptation and mutation and was the beginning of a philosophical expansion of his interest in natural history. Bergson believed that true reality is a life in continual flux, whereby 'existing consists in changing, changing in maturing, maturing in creating indefinitely oneself' (Bergson quoted in Kohler, 2008). Bergson's *élan vital* is the driving force behind this flow which generates change and variety in lifeforms and which is beyond human control. Human intellect can formalize and categorize phenomena but reality, as Bergson sees it, is not attainable to scientific intellect and therefore we cannot have a true knowledge of life. He gives the example of the different life stages – the human development from childhood to adolescence to adulthood – to show how science is limited to using abstract structuring which fails to reveal the individuality of life.

Applying Bergson's thinking to his problem of mollusk classification, Piaget reflected that if the species continue to evolve, it is 'superficial to break up the flux of life, as Bergson says, and human analysis is only a procedure, a method, based on nothing' (Piaget quoted in Kohler, 2008). Piaget would return to Bergson's philosophy during his psychological research, fundamentally basing his theory of a child's autonomous development on the concept of the *élan vital*.

Philosophy at University

Piaget's professor at university, Arnold Reymond, played a key part in Piaget's study of philosophy in much the way that Godet had in biology. Attending one of Reymond's lectures on 'The Philosophy of Bergson and the Problem of Reason' in 1913, Piaget initially reacted negatively to his professor's mathematically determined thinking, arguing that logic and mathematics could not be applied to the stages of life. However, over the next few years, Reymond was able to convince him that a strong scientific approach was vital in solving philosophical problems. Piaget would go on to use logic and mathematics in his stages of knowledge development, describing the different operations using propositional logic and mathematical group theory (see Chapter 4). Reymond's intellectual influence went further than mathematics and logic, however. He also taught epistemology (the nature of knowledge), moral philosophy, and the history of philosophy.

From the Ancients to the Enlightenment Thinkers

Interest in understanding epistemology dates back to the Ancient Greek philosophers. Aristotle (384–332 BCE) believed that our minds are born blank and that we gain knowledge through experience as we go through life. He considered the mental processes of children to be the same as adults but, as qualitatively similar younger humans, they merely had less experiences in the world which is why they had less knowledge. For Plato (c.427–346 BCE), knowledge is something that is always with us from birth to death and beyond because it resides in our eternal soul and it is simply a matter of 'reconnecting' with that knowledge through a process of thinking. These nature versus nurture perspectives continue to this day.

Another perspective however is a modification of the Aristotelian conception whereby development happens at different age-related stages of a person's life which involve clearly identifiable *structural* changes. This concept was originally put forward by the Stoics during the Hellenistic period of the early third century BCE and can be found in the writings of the Enlightenment thinker Jean-Jacques Rousseau. In his treatise on education *Émile* (1762), each chapter concentrates on a specific age period which Rousseau considered to be significant, therefore requiring a different method of teaching. Piaget takes this further in his development of a much more sophisticated stage theory which we will look at in detail in Chapter 4.

A Kantian view of epistemology is also evident in Piaget's ideas about the world. Immanuel Kant (1724–1804), an 18th-century philosopher from East Prussia (now Kaliningrad in Russia), believed that human knowledge was the product of an interaction between the individual and their environment. He believed that we impose certain structures on experience – we impose an order of cause and effect upon the way we experience the world. In other words, experience is a structuring and unifying action. Kant's categories of understanding are analogous to Piaget's idea of mental structures except that Piaget believed that these structures develop over time. This constructivist approach synthesized the empirical ideas of Aristotle with the rationalistic framework of Plato.

Kant also influenced Piaget in his study of moral development. Kant believed that we are our own moral judge and that our moral decisions come from within us. For Piaget, when children reach the more advanced stage of moral development, they achieve 'autonomous morality', which is moral reasoning based on our own rules (see Chapter 5).

A Break with Philosophy

The line between when Piaget moved away from philosophy and began to study psychology in earnest is somewhat blurred. This is perhaps because, as Piaget himself insisted, he was never fundamentally just a psychologist. His work involved sociology, epistemology, biology and philosophy of religion and science. But it was only a few years between his graduating in 1918 with hopes of being a philosopher, to his early research in children's logic in 1921. One possible reason for this change of heart may have been down to his professor, Arnold Reymond.

The same year that he graduated in 1918, Piaget published a philosophical autobiographical novel, *Recherche*, which dealt with his conflict between science and religion. It was here that he first explored his concept of equilibrium – an ideal balance between parts and the whole, both within an individual and within society. Piaget asked Reymond to write a review in one of the leading journals. However, his professor was far from complimentary, describing it as superficial and unoriginal and criticizing Piaget's philosophical theory as well as his literary and political knowledge (Kohler, 2008). This was quite a blow for Piaget, destroying any hopes he may have had for a career as a philosopher.

However, perhaps this was simply the final nail in the coffin as, in his book *Insights and Illusions of Philosophy* (1965), Piaget recounts his gradual dissatisfaction with the speculative thinking of philosophy and how this, in large part, pushed him in the direction of psychology. He wanted to back up his research on how knowledge is possible with verifiable evidence, something that philosophy could not provide.

Psychology: the Final Destination

Discussing the influences on Piaget's thinking as he changed direction must be grounded in a firm understanding of the spirit of the time regarding human psychology. Within Europe, the understanding of human behaviour was thoroughly grounded in Freudian conceptions, whereby the development of an individual repeats the history and evolutionary development of that individual's race, defining the understanding of how humans develop into the adults they become. As the world wars and racism were fomenting within Europe, many people believed that human development rested solely on genetics. This approach fuelled the eugenicist movements that contributed to the rise of Nazism in Western Europe. In America, the spirit of the times was strict behaviourism. In the early 20th century, the work of psychologist John B. Watson, which focused on the study, prediction and control of behaviour, built upon the famous studies of physiologist Ivan Pavlov (1849–1936) and his infamous salivating dogs. From there, B.F. Skinner entrenched the notions of operant conditioning indicating that human development was simply a reaction to reinforcements and punishments. While Piaget was likely influenced by Freudian, behavioural, and genetic fervour, he realized that none of the approaches adequately explained cognitive development.

When cultivating his own thoughts on development, Piaget was a confident contrarian – even from a young age – suggesting that there was more to the unfolding development of children than could be explained by any current psychological theory. Choosing to look at human development from his own perspective came about from Piaget's numerous encounters with intellectuals and children at different points along his journey to becoming a psychological scientist.

The Psychology Laboratory

Likely the most influential period of Piaget's psychological development – and the impetus for his decades-long career as a researcher of cognitive development – was his time at the psychology laboratory of the Sorbonne which was run by Alfred Binet. Having been formally trained in biology, Piaget went to Paris with the intention of becoming adept at psychological experimentation.

Prior to arriving at the psychology laboratory, Piaget had spent time working at various psychological clinics in Zurich at the same time as studying. Working with psychiatrists Carl Jung and Eugen Bleuler, he developed an interest in psychoanalysis for a brief time. This experience likely helped when he was developing the techniques he would later use for interviewing children under study (see Chapter 4).

In 1919, upon arriving at the laboratory, Piaget was assigned a seemingly uninteresting assignment of scoring standardized testing that had been administered to the children at the school next door to the laboratory. This type of work usually consists of noting whether responses to test questions are correct or incorrect, a simplistic task that does not require a high level of expertise or training. While this mundane assignment may have deterred many ambitious young scientists, in Piaget the experience ignited an insatiable desire to understand the development of knowledge over a lifespan. Binet and Simon were wholly focused on creating a test to assist the French government in helping struggling learners, but Piaget had no interest in the quantitative (numerical) scores achieved by children on IQ tests, which was the main focus of the lab. Rather, he became obsessed with understanding the qualitative (subjective) nature of their incorrect answers. Piaget noted a pattern in the way children at different ages answered the questions wrong. Convinced that the unfolding of children's intellectual abilities could be studied experimentally, he developed an informal interviewing technique to examine the reasoning behind children's incorrect answers. This realization was likely the most significant turning point in the young researcher's career and led him to consider that there was in fact a difference in how children were viewing the world at different stages of their life. Piaget's discovery in Binet's lab is likely the motivation for a program of research that fundamentally and forever changed the way society views children.

Empiricists from the 17th century had posited that the childhood brain was analogous to an adult brain with fewer connections or associations. This idea greatly influenced the perception of childhood and development for over four centuries. It was believed that children were just smaller versions of adults who simply knew less information. Psychologists didn't realize that the way in which children view the world is fundamentally different in important qualitative ways that change over time. More simply, it isn't just that children have less knowledge than adults, but that they also do not interpret the world around them in the same way. Therefore, Piaget's discovery of this seemingly obvious facet of child development was so groundbreaking that it eventually shifted the worldview of childhood. Piaget discovered that children see the world in a wholly distinct way.

Influence of Children

Piaget was fascinated by children and he enjoyed spending time with his own. In Binet's lab school, Piaget not only became captivated by children's responses in tests, but also the entertaining conversations that his numerous interactions yielded. These 'conversations' gave Piaget unusual insight into cognitive development, providing a springboard for his career path as a genetic epistemologist. This fairly unique vantage point at the outset of his academic research in psychology set the stage for everything that followed in Piaget's later career. If Piaget had not met Theodore Simon and Alfred Binet, he may never have developed insight into the thinking of young children or forever changed the way children are viewed in modern society.

Perhaps most important in any discussion of the influences on Piaget are his own three children: Jacqueline, Lucienne and Laurent. It was through countless hours of observation and note-taking of the most mundane childhood activities that Piaget became beguiled with the specification of cognitive development across childhood and adolescence. By having such long-term insight into his own children, Piaget's view of cognitive development was rare. In his encounters with children, he observed closely, writing everything down about the child, from actions to words. His highly developed semi-clinical interview method was a refreshing alternative for clinicians who felt they needed to go beyond strict adherence to standardized measures when working with very young children. His pioneering technique has yielded very fruitful results for clinicians and researchers over many decades. This in-depth interviewing technique with individual children elicits direct information into children's underlying thought processes – so simple, yet so groundbreaking for child psychology.

Piaget's Connection to Other Eminent Thinkers

Beyond the specific personal influences, Piaget stood on the shoulders of giants within the scientific realm. Zooming out and utilizing a macro-level approach to evaluate Piaget's theoretical approach, it is evident that Piaget applied ideas from other scientific fields to conceptualize his ideas about the origins of knowledge at the individual level.

To look at the field of physics from a rudimentary standpoint, the concepts from Newtonian physics were accurate for a long time until they could no longer explain anomalies within the field and the outside world. When the evidence mounted and a tipping point was realized, the field of physics underwent a profound transformation that developed into a fundamentally different, and more advanced, theoretical formulation. This enormous macro-level shift in understanding closely aligns with Piagetian descriptions of how knowledge develops at a micro-level within the individual. From the need for accommodation incited by disequilibrium (see Chapter 3) to his stages of qualitatively distinct phases of understanding, Piaget adopted ideas from the broader field of science. He drew parallels between the development of science, known as phylogeny, and the development of knowledge within individuals, known as ontology. Piaget likely borrowed this grand conceptualization from the famous assertion of German zoologist Ernst Haeckel (1834–1919) that 'ontology recapitulates phylogeny'. This famous scientific proclamation suggests that the embryonic stages of the development of organisms is parallel to the stages of that organism's evolutionary history.

Rolando Garcia

Towards the end of his academic career, Piaget co-authored a book with physicist, Rolando Garcia (1919–2012). Piaget, as a prolific scientific polymath, delighted in connections with scholars in other fields. He met Garcia through studies conducted at his International Centre for Genetic Epistemology. In their book *Psychogenesis and the History of Science* (1983), Piaget and Garcia set out to elucidate how the mechanisms of understanding transitions of the field of science are analogous to the mechanisms of individual knowledge development within humans. So, the phylogenetic (scientific) stages are equivalent to the ontogenetic (individual) stages of human knowledge acquisition. To understand the parallels between the phylogenesis and ontology, Piaget and Garcia examined physics, geometry, and algebra. They identified the mechanism that ignites change: equilibration – the vital element to understanding human development and scientific change (Tsou, 2006).

Equilibration is the autoregulation mechanism that allows any system (whether the field of science or the individual human being) to embrace new complex information into the adapted models of the past. When looking at equilibration in both cognitive development and the history of science, the main claim of Piaget and Garcia is that information from preceding stages is always integrated into the new stages. Equilibration is in effect adaptation to the environment and disequilibrium is the motivating force behind all cognitive development and scientific progress.

Basically, knowledge works in the same way as global scientific progression: when a new phenomenon is uncovered that does not fit into the existing scientific framework, disequilibrium occurs and the scientific framework is forced to adapt to fit the new information. Therefore, what Piaget and Garcia are suggesting is that the history and progression of the field of science is analogous to the individual equilibration that a human experiences (Kitchener, 1988). (See Chapter 3 for a more in depth look at equilibration and disequilibrium.)

Bärbel Inhelder

Perhaps Piaget's most important intellectual companion was his close friend, Dr. Bärbel Inhelder, an eminent psychologist and researcher in her own right. Inhelder had studied for six years at the Rousseau Institute from 1932 under the tuition of Claparède, Bovet, and Piaget, amongst others. She had then begun as an unpaid assistant and on her 20th birthday 'Piaget suggested conducting a little study, which later gained tremendous importance and inspired numerous further studies' (Inhelder quoted in Kohler, 2008). The experiment was the first in their study of reversibility (see Chapter 4). Inhelder held the role of Piaget's chief collaborator for over five decades, co-writing books and articles and being a sounding board for ideas regarding cognitive development. Her ideas specifically influenced Piaget's notions about the formal operational period of development (described in Chapter 3). In fact, Inhelder is credited with discovering the formal operations, as her initial experiments helped conceptualize a more nuanced understanding of children's perceptions and conservation abilities. Some of the many works that Piaget and Inhelder completed together include *The Child's Construction of Physical Quantities* (1942), *The Growth of Logical Thinking from Childhood to Adolescence* (1958), *Child's Conception of Space* (1963) and *The Psychology of the Child* (1969). While Piaget and Inhelder worked closely together until Piaget's death, Inhelder's research and interests veered away and took a more applied approach in later years.

Behaviourism as an Anti-influence

The first barrier to widespread acceptance of Piaget ideas and his approach to research was language, with his works taking decades to be translated into English. There were also additional, more philosophical, barriers for Piaget to surmount in order to become mainstream in the developing field of psychology and educational research. The overarching approach to research in the psychological domain was dominated by the behaviourist tradition in the early to mid-20th century, especially in the United States. Piaget's ideas regarding how to study human development were therefore particularly foreign. Piaget wanted to deviate from the simplistic and mechanistic nature of behaviourism to develop a more comprehensive and individual understanding of human behaviour and development, and so he rebelled against it.

The leading behavioural psychologists of the time – B.F. Skinner, Edward Thorndike (1874–1949), and John B. Watson – posited that only observable and measurable behaviours could be studied scientifically within the realm of psychology. To them, trying to uncover what occurred inside the 'black box' of the human mind was a pointless endeavour. The core concepts of Piagetian psychology – deeply entrenched in the later-developing ideas emanating from the cognitive revolution – were more alien than the French language they were written in. Piaget's main focus was on the underlying mental processes of the human mind in direct opposition to the studies of the popular behaviourists of the time.

Beyond the focus of observable and measurable data, the dominant American behavioural psychologists insisted upon rigorous experimental methods that contrasted with Piaget's qualitative case study approach to understanding the developing child. Piaget did not use hypothesis testing and control groups, instead he developed a clinical-descriptive technique that became a distinctive component of his research (Woodsworth, 2004). While Piaget's methods did not resemble the psychological research of the strict behaviourists, his observational methods were methodical and detailed, providing evidence of small developmental changes of the subjects of his many investigations.

Piaget's research trademark was his method of interviewing children. Described as semi-clinical interviews, Piaget's interactions with children were often led by a combination of the child's responses and Piaget's own intuition, an approach that some scientists criticized as unscientific. Despite this, Piaget was able to uncover facets of human development that would not have been discovered using structured behaviourist approaches under standardized conditions. Within the Piagetian realm of research, no two subjects (children) ever received the same conditions, which is anathema to many of his behavioural psychology peers who were determined to uncover universal scientific truths about human and animal behaviour.

Through this deviating approach to psychological research, Piaget was able to discover detailed understanding of cognitive, social, and emotional development across infancy and childhood. In response to criticism, Piaget and his colleagues countered that each of their subjects were individual longitudinal designs that encompassed years of observation of small groups of children. Because of the longitudinal nature of much of Piaget's work, the small sample sizes were suitable for developmental research.

While much of the vast array of Piaget's research was dominated by small sample sizes, he did use traditional techniques for later works. *The Early Growth of Logic in the Child: Classification and Seriation* (1964) and *The Mechanisms of Perception* (1969) both apply appropriate statistical procedures and sample sizes. Despite the incessant denunciation of his research methodology, Piaget was able to reveal previously unknown facets of human knowledge acquisition. Therefore, even his greatest detractors had to acknowledge that the systematic nature of his long-term observations of children were conducted in a rigorous way that yielded fascinatingly compelling contributions to the field of psychology.

Piaget the Polymath

Piaget was a profoundly important thinker in the underlying philosophy of psychological science. His unique background experiences and professional relationships with scholars in varying disciplines, in addition to his close ties to his own children's development, allowed him to view the world of human development through an exceptional vantage point. His training in the hard sciences combined with his lifelong interactions with scientists across many fields of study propelled him to see things in the field of psychology that no other great thinker had realized, which made his ideas revolutionary. Piaget was able to develop his complicated epistemology and then have it translated to usable ideas within the fields of education and psychology. This practical legacy had been an enduring phenomenon that continues into the present day.

3. The Organization of Knowledge

'What the genetic epistemology proposes is discovering the roots of the different varieties of knowledge, since its elementary forms, following to the next levels, including also the scientific knowledge.' Piaget, 1970

Piaget's intense interest relating to how organisms adapt to changes in environmental conditions began with his early fascination with mollusks as a child and continued with his experiences as a biologist and his observations of the natural world. Then, when spending time administering intelligence tests in Alfred Binet's laboratory in Geneva, Piaget became consumed with understanding the basic structures of human knowledge.

Genetic epistemology literally means the genesis of knowledge. Piaget did not consider himself a developmental psychologist, but rather a genetic epistemologist. Knowing this allows insight into Piaget's understanding of his research pursuits over several decades by framing his view of the world as someone on a quest to understand how humans acquire and develop their base of knowledge and how knowledge structures are organized and transformed.

The Puzzle

Piaget stated, 'Genetic epistemology attempts to explain knowledge, and in particular scientific knowledge, on the basis of its history, its sociogenesis, and especially the psychological origins and operations upon which it is based' (1970a). The main puzzle of genetic epistemology, according to Piaget, revolves around the mechanisms that function to transform rudimentary forms of knowledge into more sophisticated arrangements of information. In other words, what instigates the movement from the relatively low-resolution world of a young child to higher and higher levels of resolution in adolescence and beyond? Why do children respond in different ways than adults when posed with the same question?

With his training in the biological sciences, Piaget determined that biological acts are adaptation to the physical environment which help systematically organize the environment (Wadsworth, 2004). With Piaget's transition to the world of psychology, he began to see the similarities between the physical body and the mind, which led him to postulate that intellectual development is organized similarly to biological development – as acts of organization and adaptation. In fact, Piaget contemplated that intellectual functioning is a distinctive form of biological activity (Wadsworth, 2004). He believed that just as the stomach, heart, and lungs are biological structures that adapt to their environment, so too are the psychological structures that humans develop to adapt and change as they grow older.

Constructivism

Piaget adopted a constructivist approach to knowledge development meaning that he believed the individual to be at the centre of knowledge construction and acquisition. Piaget spent so much time observing his own children through the lens of a scientist, he realized that learning is based upon a child's natural desire to sense, explore, and master the world around them. Instead of forcing children to be passive recipients of knowledge, Piaget felt that the fundamental notion of development should be focused around letting children construct their own knowledge by using this natural curiosity about the world. Therefore, says Piaget, development is an active rather than a passive process, defined by the organism interacting with and interpreting the world.

Piaget believed that a true independent reality exists in which every developing human gains a clearer more accurate representation of the surrounding world as they age. The constructivism Piaget espoused suggests that children construct knowledge via exploratory actions on their environment. Manipulations of objects (physical actions) and wondering about something (mental actions) are both considered to be examples of knowledge construction. If a child's interest is piqued then exploration follows; he then tries to fit the information into his current knowledge base or alter his knowledge base if it does not fit. This process of active learning came to be known as constructivism.

This active role was a conceptual shift away from the passive role that an individual plays in the behaviourist model wherein the child is merely responding to environmental cues of reinforcement and punishment.

Five Epistemological Concepts

Piaget developed five basic cognitive conceptualizations to illustrate the development of human knowledge acquisition:

schema, assimilation, accommodation, equilibration, and constructivism (which we looked at above). All relate to the overarching concept of adaptation to the environment – a topic of interest that leads back to Piaget's original study of mollusks in Swiss lakes during his childhood (see Chapter 1). These concepts are applicable across age spans and provide clear insight into Piaget's view of the developing mind. For Piaget, 'The current state of knowledge is a moment in history, changing just as rapidly as the state of knowledge in the past has ever changed and, in many instances, more rapidly.' (Piaget, 1968)

Schemas

A schema (plural schemata or schemas) is a way of organizing distinct pieces of knowledge within the human mind. Each particular schema that an individual human has is a representation related to different aspects of the world – objects, abstractions, concepts and actions. In 2004, renowned Piaget scholar William Wadsworth suggested that schemas could be conceptualized as an index card filing system within the brain. Each index card contains information regarding how an individual should approach or react to a given concept or category. Each schema is akin to a unit of knowledge.

As with most of Piaget's ideas, schemas relate to his understanding of the world based on his training as a biologist. His description of knowledge structures within the human mind corresponds to biological structures within the human body. To Piaget, schemas are the basic building blocks of all knowledge. These theoretical mental structures by which individual humans organize their world allow us to make sense of the past and plan for the future. In 1952, Piaget defined schema as, 'a cohesive, repeatable action sequence possessing component actions that are tightly interconnected and governed by a core meaning.'

Adults have a large filing system with many index cards (schemas), but when a child is born, there are very few cards on file. As a child ages and experiences the world, the filing system grows both quantitively, in terms of number of index cards, but also qualitatively in terms of the kinds of information and the level of detail on each of the index cards. Schemas continually become more and more refined as humans age. For example, a young child may have a schema for dog as they are commonly seen in daily life. The child may learn that different types of animals fit into the dog schema. They would add information to their card based on experience and a set of common characteristics of the animal – four-legged, friendly, and playful.

A schema does not just refer to a tangible object, like a dog. Humans create schemas for more complicated conceptualizations, such as how to go shopping or drive a car. These types of schemas would be akin to a script. When a person walks into the grocery store or gets into their car, the script for these actions would be activated. Schemas are fundamentally concepts or categories that humans use to organize and structure their experiences in the world. As children develop, they continually fine tune their schemas and as they do so their perception of the world becomes more accurate.

According to Piaget, even newborn babies have innate – albeit very rudimentary – knowledge structures that appear to be genetically programmed reflexive cognitive structures. These innate reflexive schemas include sucking, grasping, and rooting. Newborn babies will reflexively suck on whatever is put in front of them but then, as weeks pass, they develop more than one sucking schema, understanding that sometimes sucking results in milk and other times it does not. This differentiation, according to Piaget, is not the same as the later development of schemas but is a reflexive response which comes from the newborn's limited ability to understand the environment. Over time, as the infant develops into a child, the filing system becomes more intricate with many more index cards in the file box.

As children grow, schemas become considerably more complex. The foundation of schemas changes from being related to physical activity to more functional and conceptual properties. Eventually the schemas relate to abstractions about objects, events, and ideas. They are constantly modified and adapt as the child interacts with the environment and guides their own intellectual growth. There are two processes constantly working together to drive the progression of intellectual development: assimilation and accommodation. When these two mechanisms are working well, equilibration is the result and the developing child navigates the world without significant qualitative changes in cognitive development. When the two mechanisms are out of balance, disequilibrium propels the child to a wholly different view of the world. (We will look at this in more detail in Chapter 4.)

Assimilation

Assimilation is the process of integrating new experiences into already existing schemas – without modification. A simple example would be of a baby who learns to grasp an object. The infant will quickly use their grasping schema to integrate in new information and try to grasp toys, balls, and other small objects. The construct of assimilation is formally defined as the 'cognitive process by which a person integrates new perceptual, motor, or conceptual matter into existing schemata or patterns of behavior' (Wadsworth, 2004). Like many of Piaget's ideas about the underlying processes contributing to cognitive development, he borrowed ideas for the process of assimilation from the fields of biology.

Assimilation occurs continually as environmental information is taken in from the outside world and mapped on to existing schemas. For example, a young child is walking along with his parents and sees a Border Collie and correctly says, 'doggy'. His parents are proud that he recognizes it as a dog and give him positive reinforcements. Even though he has never seen that particular breed of dog before, he knows that it is similar to the other four-legged creature that lives in his house. So, he correctly places the information onto his 'doggy' index card – an example of assimilation.

While assimilation accounts for significant quantitative developmental growth, it does not account for changes in existing schemas. To understand the changes that occur and motivate children to understand new information about their world, Piaget describes the process of accommodation.

Accommodation

Sometimes, when a child encounters a new phenomenon or stimulus, the novel information does not fit into an existing schema and the child must figure out how to interpret and process the new information. There are basically two courses of action for the child at this point. The first option is for the child to determine if the existing related schema can be adapted to fit the new information from the outside world. The second option would be to create an entirely new index card – a newly created schema. Piaget considers both options to be different formulations of accommodation, which is the creation of new schemas or the modification of old schemas. The end result of either action is change in cognitive structures, which would be defined as cognitive development. Put simply, accommodation occurs when schemas are modified in any way based on experience in the world.

For example, a very young child may see a horse while walking along a path with her parents. She may look at it – seeing it for the first time – and assume it is a dog, which is the four-legged creature she is most used to seeing in her everyday life. The parents likely correct her and tell her it is a horse and perhaps give her more information about what a horse is like compared to a dog. So initially, the young girl would likely try to file the animal on the dog mental 'index card'. When, over time, she learns that it does not belong on that card, she will need to create a new index card for horse. While she tried to fit it into her existing schema, parental input helped her realize that it was a different animal altogether. According to Piaget, children going through the processes of accommodation and assimilation are actively constructing their understanding of the world. This facet is key to understanding the overarching Piagetian ideas centred around development. That is, cognitive development is an active, rather than passive, process in which the child must be a participant in order to construct their own reality. These constructions are a representation of the child's particular understanding of the world and do not necessarily reflect an accurate representation of reality, but as the children develop, their view of the world more closely aligns with reality.

Practically, behaviour is unlikely all assimilation or accommodation, but rather reflects a combination of both (Wadsworth, 2004). A child imposing his current available knowledge structure on a situation would be 'assimilating', while a child who is forced to change her knowledge structure in response to a given situation would be 'accommodating'. We can see why Piaget's developmental theory was so groundbreaking: it changed the concept of a child. Whereas before children were seen as 'mini-adults' who made only quantitative cognitive changes over time (assimilation), Piaget presented a much clearer picture that encapsulated the realization that children undergo significant qualitative changes in thought (accommodation). The continued alternation between these two theoretical processes drives new understanding of the world.

Equilibrium

As a child navigates the world the cognitive processes of assimilation and accommodation are both necessary functions that ignite cognitive development. According to Piaget, when a child's existing schemas are predominantly able to explain the world, then they are said to be in equilibrium. This is a state of cognitive mental balance that is self-regulating and assures optimal interaction with the environment. It is an inner sense of balance between the child's old and new thoughts. During this state of relative cognitive calm, the world makes sense as the child glides through the world; accommodation and equilibration are stable. Problems occur when an existing schema cannot acclimate new information. This situation pushes the child into a state of disequilibrium: a state of tension and stress in which a mental change needs to take place to propel the individual back towards equilibration.

This tension is the key to understanding the developmental philosophy of Piaget. A child in disequilibrium is motivated to strive towards equilibration because of the cognitive stress they are experiencing. To accomplish this, the child must increase assimilation or accommodation, with the end goal always being a striving towards equilibration and ultimately assimilation into either a new or old schema. Importantly, assimilation is always the end goal and sometimes the child's placement of information does not fit into the appropriate schema (according to adult understanding). However, the child's placement of the information is always appropriate for whatever her understanding of the world is at that point in time.

Equilibration is the theoretical process that drives cognitive development. It interacts with maturation, the physical environment, and the social environment to ignite developmental change in a synergistic unfolding. These processes are the engine that propels cognitive development and a key to understanding how humans learn and grow from a cognitive perspective. According to Piaget, humans are always seeking a state of equilibrium, but schemas are constantly undergoing disequilibrium, growth, and change as the organism (child) adapts to her surroundings.

This process of equilibration continues throughout all levels of cognitive development, from infancy through to adulthood. The constructed knowledge gets acted upon by either the process of assimilation or accommodation, with a drive to keep the individual (organism, as Piaget described) in balance. Humans are continually in the process of adaptation to the world around them.

Assimilation and accommodation are usually in balance, or equilibrium, meaning that at most points in time, children are assimilating most information, while occasionally needing to accommodate. Here is an example of a young child assimilating and accommodating with ease:

> *'When John, an energetic 2 1/2-year-old, saw a monarch butterfly for the first time, his mother, Patrice, told him, "Butterfly, butterfly; that's a butterfly, John." A few minutes later a zebra swallowtail landed on a nearby bush and John shouted in excitement, "Butterfly, Mama, butterfly!" A bit later, a moth flew out of another bush; with even greater excitement in his voice, John shouted, "Butterfly, Mama, more butterfly!" As Patrice was telling John, "No honey, that's a moth, not a butterfly," she marveled at how rapidly John seemed to grasp new concepts with so little direction from her.'* (Kail, 1998)

At a certain point along the developmental trajectory, children become unbalanced and more accommodation than assimilation is needed, which causes cognitive tension that may become so overwhelming that the child's fundamental view of the world needs significant altering. This discomfort pushes the child into an entirely new stage of development.

A detailed description of Piaget's Stage Theory will be discussed in the next chapter.

4. Stages of Cognitive Development

'Knowledge [...] is a system of transformations that become progressively adequate.' (Piaget quoted in Bringuier, 1980)

Throughout human history, it has been assumed that children are miniature versions of adults. In the 1930s, Jean Piaget altered this viewpoint dramatically with his groundbreaking theory: the first comprehensive and systematic description of cognitive development. While evaluating children in Alfred Binet's IQ lab (see Chapter 2), Piaget realized that intellectual reasoning in early childhood is fundamentally different than in later childhood and adolescence. In addition, he noticed that children within fairly consistent age groupings appear to have similar *incorrect* answers to questions. This similarity intrigued Piaget and led to his ideas regarding cognitive development.

Fundamentally, Piaget noted that the discrepancy between incorrect and correct answers is more than a quantitative increase in knowledge over time. Instead, according to Piaget, the cognitive disparities between children at various ages seems to be qualitative in nature, with a fundamental reorganization of cognitive structures appearing to occur in stages.

What Does This Mean?

How younger children answer questions seems to undergo radical transformations at certain stages of their development. This realization led to Piaget's formulation of his stage-based theory of cognitive development. The stages proposed by Piaget span from infancy through to adolescence. At birth, infants' knowledge of the world is limited. Their unfolding physical development is spurred by gradually increasing motor activity which then kindles their cognitive growth. From infancy, children then move into more complex thinking patterns via a synergy between biological maturation and environmental input. The movement through each of the stages is unchanging, but the ages that individual children pass through each stage is variable.

Challenging the behavioural theories that dominated much of psychology during the early 20th century, Piaget did not believe that children were born as blank slates. Nor did he agree with the eugenicists who championed the genetic influence of intelligence. Piaget's unique perspective as a trained biologist turned psychologist led him to recognize that biological development drives cognitive development via interactions with the environment. This interaction between biological growth and environmental stimulus pushes the child towards more advanced levels of thinking until a peak is reached. It is at this point that individuals can reason abstractly by understanding and manipulating information that is not in the here and now.

Piaget's stage theory of intellectual development includes the following four stages:

Sensorimotor Stage: infancy (0 to 2 years)

Preoperational Stage: preschool and early elementary school years: (2 to 7 years)

Concrete Operational Stage: middle and late elementary years (7 to 11 years)

Formal Operational Stage: adolescence and adulthood (11 years and older)

Sensorimotor Stage

From birth through to approximately two years of age, infants and toddlers primarily interact with the world through sensory modalities and the manipulation of objects. During the earliest part of this stage, most of the interaction is via basic innate reflexes and sensory-motor responses. As any parent will attest, the growth in cognitive development at this time is dramatic. By continuously interacting with the world around them, infants and toddlers learn and make important, yet basic, discoveries about how the world works. For this short period of time, the growth is incredible. Actions such as crawling and walking, and leaps in both receptive and expressive language, unfold during this stage.

Piaget further identified six substages of the sensorimotor stage (see Fig. 10). Piaget noted that, although infants move through the stages in the same order, there is significant variation in the timing that each child reaches each stage (as every child is different). However, most children achieve each stage within the time frame suggested by Piaget. It is therefore important to recognize that these age ranges are to be thought of as approximations for each stage.

Sub-Stage	Age (mths)	Accomplishment	Example
Simple Reflexes	0-1	Reflexes become coordinated	Sucking a nipple
Primary Circular Reactions	1-4	An infant's first learned adaptations to the world	Thumb sucking
Secondary Tertiary Reactions	4-8	Allowing infants to learn about objects	Shaking a toy to hear it rattle
Coordination of Reactions	8-12	Onset of intentional behaviour	Moving an obstacle to reach a toy
Tertiary Circular Reactions	12-18	Children begin to experiment	Shaking different toys to hear the sounds they make
Early Symbolic Thought	18-24	Symbolic processing appears in language, gestures, and pretend play	Eating pretend food with a pretend spoon

Fig 10 Table showing the six substages of the sensorimotor stage (adapted from Kail, 1998).

The primary focus of the sensorimotor stage for infants and young toddlers is the acquisition of knowledge through sensory experiences and manipulation of objects. One of the main accomplishments of the sensorimotor stage is the development of object permanence: the understanding that objects continue to exist, even after they are out of sight. Younger infants get great joy out of simple games of peek-a-boo. Within a short time, older infants are no longer amused as they understand their playmate still exists, even hidden behind a blanket. Piaget's supposition was that all concepts are developed and not innate like basic instinctual reflexes. He felt the child must construct his own world through experiences, a fundamental facet of all of Piaget's thought on cognitive development.

Beyond the eventual development of object permanence in the first year of life, another major accomplishment is the coordination of intentional behaviour. Time spent around a very young infant indicates that little behaviour in the first month goes beyond instinct into deliberate movement. However, a month or two after birth, purely reflexive behaviours begin to be modified and new behaviours start to appear. A common occurrence during this period is intentional thumb-sucking that is made possible by rapid development of motoric coordination. While the thumb-sucking behaviour is originally accidental, it slowly develops into intentional and habitual action as Piaget writes,

> *'When the child systematically sucks his thumb, no longer due to chance contacts but through coordination between hand and mouth, this may be called acquired accommodation. Neither the reflexes of the mouth nor of the hand can be provided such coordination by heredity (there is no instinct to suck the thumb!) and experience alone explains its formation.'* (Piaget, 1952)

Another development during this stage is the movement of the infant towards the ability to reproduce interesting events. Infants begin replicating incidents that interest them. As with the above example, Piaget documented this cognitive unfolding via observation of his own son, Laurent,

> *'Observation 104.—At 03;(29) Laurent grasps a paper knife which he sees for the first time; he looks at it a moment and then swings it while holding it in his right hand. During these movements the object happens to rub against the wicker of the bassinet. Laurent then waves his arms vigorously and obviously tries to reproduce*

> *the sound he has heard, but without understanding the necessity of contact between the paper and the wicker and, consequently, without achieving this contact otherwise by chance.*
>
> *At 0;4(3) same reactions, but Laurent looks at the object at the time when it happens to rub against the wicker of the bassinet. The same still occurs at 0;4(5) but there is slight progress towards systemization.*
>
> *Finally, at 0;4(6) the movement becomes intentional; as soon as the child has the object in his hand, he rubs it with regularity against the wicker of the bassinet.'* (Piaget, 1952)

These examples of sensorimotor milestones epitomize Piaget's detailed observations of his own children which led to his innovative theories about some of the underlying universal principles of cognitive development.

According to Piaget, for the first several months of infancy the infant believes that he is solely responsible for the causes of all activity. It is not until around 8 to 12 months that infants begin to show awareness that other 'objects' can be the cause of outside activities. He states,

> *'The cause of a certain phenomenon is no longer identified by the child with the feeling he has of acting upon the phenomenon. The subject begins to discover that a spatial contact exists between cause and effect and so any object at all can be a source of activity (and not only his own body).'* (Piaget, 1952)

Overview of Sensorimotor Stage

By age two years, most children have made earth-shattering transformations in all areas, but especially in terms of cognitive development. As a newborn and early infant, most of the child's behaviour is innately reflexive, relating to instinctual processes. As months go by, motor coordination develops rapidly and the infants begin to better understand the surrounding world.

The culmination of the sensorimotor stage is the development of symbolic thought, with most infants well on their way to talking and gesturing about the world as words and actions stand for something else. Many children at this stage also begin to develop a fondness for pretend play, with a huge explosion in imaginative thinking. Children generally have an eruption of language and use more complicated words and phrasing as they navigate the world. While the growth in this stage is remarkable, children are only able to see the world in very concrete terms and they commonly have difficulty fully understanding the perspectives of others. Reasoning at this stage is based almost entirely upon individual perception of the world, so it is not yet logical in orientation.

Preoperational Stage

Piaget was fascinated by the behaviour of children in the next stage of development – the preoperational stage: 'One of the most striking things one finds about the child under 7–8 is his extreme assurance on all subjects.' (Piaget, 1928)

Perhaps Piaget's biggest claim to fame was the experiments he conducted with children during the preoperational stage that elucidated just how very different their view of the world is compared to adults. His most famous experiments with children centre around the principles of egocentrism, centration, conservation, reversibility, and appearance as reality. Children at this stage (approximately ages two to seven years old) are developing more and more advanced levels of symbolic representation. They use symbols such as language, drawings, and objects to represent ideas – a major shift from sensorimotor cognition. For example, a child holding a banana and talking into it – pretending it is a phone – would be using cognitive capacities that are emblematic of the preoperational stage of thought.

Egocentrism

While the advancement of thought that occurs during the preoperational stage is remarkable, there are still significant limitations and vast qualitative differences between cognition during this stage and late adolescence and adulthood. A major facet of this stage is a child's individualistic thinking patterns that Piaget labelled egocentrism. This refers to young children being unable to see the world from another person's point of view, believing that everyone sees the same world and thinks the same way. There is no motivation to question one's own thinking at this stage, even when presented with contradictory evidence. The egocentric thought is not vindictive or purposeful, but simply a reflection of cognitive capacities and children typically conclude other people are wrong when they do not agree with them.

Children at this stage often talk to themselves, even in the presence of others. Generally there is not a vast exchange between individuals, but rather a one-sided conversation with little developed interaction. Typically, around age six or seven, children become more aware that their thoughts may be in conflict with other individuals and they begin to adjust to others and determine who is correct. Social conflict actually pushes young children to disequilibrium (see Chapter 3) and to look for verification of their own thoughts. The disequilibrium ignites movement and adaptation to the outside world.

While egocentrism is a foundational cognitive assumption at this stage, Piaget and later scholars have noted that this cognitive limitation is often present in later stages, but to a lesser extent. Even into adulthood, examples of egocentric thought abound. However, according to Piaget, within the preoperational child the pervasiveness of egocentrism limits cognitive development and therefore must be overcome to move on to the next stage.

Centration

Children in the preoperational stage of cognitive development tend to centre or fixate their attention on one aspect of a situation or object. Instead of exploring the entirety of a stimulus, children exhibit what Piaget labelled 'centration'. To evaluate the centration aspect of children's thinking, Piaget developed tasks to understand the principle of conservation (logical thinking ability) among children in the preoperational stage (see Fig 11).

A child of about four years of age may be presented with two sets of coins in a row. One row contains ten coins and the other row contains nine coins. However, the nine-coin row may be spread out with much more space between each coin and so it appears longer. When asked which row has more coins, the preoperational child will insist the longer row has more coins. Even when the child understands that ten is more than nine and they count each of the coins, they will stick to their belief due to their centration on the length of the rows as the most prominent aspect of the

Type of Conservation	Initial Presentation	Starting Configuration Question	Transformation	Final Configuration Question
Liquid quantity	Two glasses of water of equal shape and size	Is there the same amount of water in each glass?	Pour water from one glass to another taller, narrower glass	Now is there the same amount of water in each glass, or does one have more?
Number	Two lines of pennies of equal amount	Are there the same number of pennies in each row?	Stretch out the top row of pennies; push together the bottom row	Now are there the same number of pennies in each row, or does one have more?
Length	Two sticks of equal length	Does each ball have the same amount of clay?	Roll one ball so that it looks like a sausage	Now does each piece have the same amount of clay, or does one have more?
Mass	Two balls of clay of equal amount	Does each ball have the same amount of clay?	Roll one ball so that it looks like a sausage	Now does each piece have the same amount of clay, or does one have more?
Area	Two piles of grass of equal amount	Does each cow have the same amount of grass to eat?	Spread one of the piles of grass out	Now does each cow have the same amount to eat, or does one have more?

Fig. 11 Five tasks that Piaget used to understand the principle of conservation (adapted from Kail, 1994).

stimulus. One of Piaget's most famous experiments asks children to watch liquid being poured from a short fat container to a taller skinnier container and then indicate which container has more. Preoperational children choose the taller container despite seeing the movement of the water with their own eyes. They fixate on the height of the container and are unable to move past that particular property to accurately answer the question.

Reversibility

Piaget felt that reversibility – following a line of reasoning back to where it started – is the most clearly defined characteristic of intelligence. In the previous examples regarding understanding the conservation tasks, a young child in the preoperational stage would not be able to understand the concept of reversibility even though she saw the original (starting) configurations. This is because she would be unable to mentally work backwards and reverse the actions. While preoperational thought is significantly more flexible that sensorimotor thought, the limitations are apparent and the attainment of reversibility is a significant challenge for the developing child.

Appearance as Reality

Another core component of preoperational children's thought is that the appearance of an object always indicates what the object is really like. For example, an older child putting a mask on and surprising a five-year-old would likely create a frightening situation for the younger child, who would not quite understand that the older child is actually just his sibling with a mask on. This confusion between appearance and reality can extend beyond masks to misunderstanding facial expressions that do not align with what another person is actually feeling. Or to being unaware that blue-tinted glasses are changing the way things appear, but as soon as the glasses are taken off, everything will be back to normal (and never changed to begin with). While initially many researchers were skeptical, experiments have repeatedly replicated Piaget's findings, indicating that the confusion between appearance and reality is an entrenched portion of preoperational thought, especially in the earliest years of this stage.

Summary of Preoperational Thought

Children in the preoperational stage have significant cognitive advantages as compared to those in the earlier sensorimotor stage.

Children are able to move beyond thoughts that are restricted to immediate perceptual and motor events to more advanced levels of symbolic representation. However, the main driver of thought at this stage is nevertheless perception, as logical thought has not yet developed. When a conflict between thought and reality does appear, preoperational children fall back on what their perception tells them rather than trying to apply logic to the outside world. Despite the limitation noted, preoperational children make huge advancements in language, and conversational skills begin to develop into more communicative and social behaviour.

Concrete Operational Stage

At around age seven, many children begin to enter a new stage of cognitive development that begins to contain more elements that correspond to later adult thought. This stage, labelled the 'concrete operational stage' by Piaget, generally spans from age 7 to 11, although there is variability in the age estimates. At this point a child's underlying cognitive framework undergoes radical change for the first time, beginning to use mental operations to solve problems. This new approach encompasses strategies and rules that make the child's thinking more powerful and systematic.

A simple example of this newfound ability is the application of mathematical operations. Addition, subtraction, multiplication, and division are all operations that elementary school children slowly begin to understand and apply. The development of these mental operations allows children to use a rule-based, logical orientation to thought that is absent in the pre-operational child. Piaget defines these logical mental operations as an 'internalized system of actions that is fully reversible' (Piaget, 1981). At this stage, most children are able to follow a line of reasoning back to where it started.

The concrete operational child has no trouble solving the conservation tasks described earlier. They do not fall victim to centration and they are able to provide correct reasoning for their answers. Furthermore, when a child in the concrete operational stage is presented with a conflict between their thoughts and perception, they are able to use reason to attempt to discern the discrepancy. Significant advances in language are also apparent, with the concrete operational child becoming much less egocentric and more socially communicative, frequently engaging in give-and-take conversations with peers and adults. While the cognitive advances are numerous, there are still significant limitations as the newly developed logical processes are only applicable to real and observable (concrete) phenomena. The major limitation of this stage is that children are not yet able to apply their logical thought to hypothetical or abstract conceptualizations.

Another major advancement of the concrete operational stage is the realization of the importance of rules in game-playing and cooperating in social group settings. No longer is there a completely rigid adherence to rules; a more nuanced understanding of rules begins to materialize that shows the child's emergence of cognitive flexibility that was not present in the preoperational stage. Children start to understand that often cooperation with others leads to changes in rules that make more logical sense for a particular situation.

A more complex view of honesty, truth, and justice emerges at the end of the concrete operational stage, with children beginning to understand the gradations of lying and laws. At around age 10 or 11, most children begin to understand the intentions behind lying and to judge lies differently based on particular situations. Justice is seen as fixed and unchangeable in the preoperational child, but the concrete operational child applies more adult-like considerations to how justice should be applied depending on a particular infringement (see Chapter 5 for a more in-depth look at a child's moral development).

Summary of Concrete Operational Stage

Huge advancements in cognition occur as children pass through the concrete operational stage of Piaget's theory. This stage provides the child with a much more powerful and accurate framework to view the world. However, many limitations still exist. Logical thought, while developed in the concrete operational child, is still limited to the here and now – the tangible and real in the child's environment. At this point, a child is not yet able to employ the powerful cognitive processes of hypothetical and deductive reasoning.

Formal Operational Stage

Around age 11 or 12, most individuals begin to apply hypothetical-deductive reasoning to problem-solving, and mental operations to abstract ideas. This profound change allows the older child to understand that all thought does not have to be reality-bound. Wherein the foundation of concrete operational thought is reality, the formal operational child can begin to hypothesize about unknown alternatives to more complicated problems and situations that they may not have experienced in the physical world.

The formal operational child is able to initiate the creation and testing out of hypotheses to solve problems. They are able to apply more advanced levels of logic to hypothetical situations. In addition, as individuals enter adolescence, they start to make more sophisticated attempts at reaching conclusions from known information via a process of deductive reasoning. A classic example of an experiment that a formal operational child would pass, but a concrete operational child would fail is as follows:

> A child is told the following rule: 'If you hit a glass with a hammer, the glass will break.'
>
> They are then asked: 'If Jane hit a glass with a hammer, what would happen?'

Children in both the concrete operational and formal operational stages grasp that this rule is logical. Therefore they would respond with, 'The glass broke'. For concrete operational children, this response is likely due to their experiences: when you hit something made of glass with a hard object, the glass will break. However, when posed with the following rule and question, the responses of children at the different stages diverge:

> A child is told the following rule: 'If you hit a glass with a feather, the glass will break'.
>
> They are then asked: 'If Jane hit a glass with a feather, what would happen?'

In this example, the scenario doesn't make literal sense, so the younger concrete operational child would be confused. As the conclusion that follows is counterfactual to experience (they have never had concrete experience with breaking a glass with a soft object) the child would likely respond that the glass wouldn't break as the feather is soft. However, for the older formal operational child, they are able to relate back to the rule that the feather will break the glass – after all, a rule is a rule – and, understanding the hypothetical nature of this abstract problem, they will be able to respond correctly that the glass would break, based on the rule presented.

This newly developed formal operational thought is a powerful mechanism for understanding the world. Children who have developed this more advanced orientation take an abstract, hypothetical approach towards problem-solving. Rather than being constrained by reality, like children in the concrete operational stage, these more advanced thinkers are open to different alternatives and possibilities. Related to this ability to contemplate beyond the here and now, is the typical path of adolescence which includes experimentation with unconventional beliefs and lifestyles.

One of the fundamental precepts of scientific thought is the ability to reason inductively, moving from specific facts to general conclusions. This is the main driver of science and how scientists create generalities and laws. The ability to think about numerous variables at a time allows individuals in the formal operational stage to reason in a coordinated manner. Referred to as combinatorial reasoning, Piaget found that this ability was something most children in the concrete operational stage could not do reliably.

Piaget also used analogies to differentiate between individuals who had reached formal operations and those who had not yet done so. To Piaget, the ability to understand and correctly identify an analogy only comes through what he termed 'reflective abstraction'. That is, the relationship that is uncovered in an analogy cannot be deduced from direct concrete experiences in the world. For example, a simple purpose analogy would be 'pen is to writer as voice is to singer'.

Once adolescents reach the stage of formal operations, according to Piaget, their final cognitive developmental stage has been reached. Despite this, adolescents and adults alike continue to gain knowledge across multiple domains as they age, but the fundamental mechanisms of thought – the structures of knowledge – remain the same throughout the remainder of the life span. After the culmination of this stage there are no more structural enhancements in the quality of reasoning, only in the quantitative increase of knowledge. More specifically, while the mechanisms of assimilation and accommodation continue throughout the life span in reaction to disequilibrium and further changes to schemas, these changes are only in regard to the amount of knowledge. Importantly, while Piaget initially believed that most people reach formal operational thought by the time they are in late adolescence, later studies suggest that as many as 50 percent of the American population may never reach this more cognitively advanced mode of thinking (Elkind, 1962). It is unknown why many adults do not reach formal abstract thought, but it may be due to a combination of intellectual and environmental variability among adults.

Summary of Formal Operational Stage

According to Piaget the stage of formal operations typically begins around age 12 and continues to build upon, integrate, and extend the intellectual structures established during concrete operations. While most children below age 12 are restricted to applying logical problem-solving to the here and now, formal operations allow the individual to move beyond their own experiences in the world to imagine the 'what-if'. This transformation is the final major structural cognitive change that occurs in human development, according to Piaget. While individuals still continue to learn and increase their funds of knowledge, the methods used to understand the world remain similar throughout the life span.

Overview of Stage Theory

The concept of fixed stages of development that occur in a universal order may be Piaget's most lasting idea. Here he explains,

> *'the stages of cognitive development that a child passes through on the way to adulthood are universally sequential—so that each stage is at once the result of possibilities opened up by the preceding stage and a necessary condition for the following one [...] each stage begins with a reorganization, at another level, of the principal acquisitions that occurred at the preceding stages.'* (Piaget & Garcia, 1983)

While Piaget continually – and insistently – stated that the stages occur in a constant order rather than at a fixed age, many educators have persistently mis-interpreted Piaget's writings, suggesting he asserted that the ages themselves were fixed and universal. Cross-cultural studies conducted over time have generally shown that there is a universality of sequence of

Piaget's Four Stages of Cognitive Development

Stage	Approximate Age	Major Characteristics
Sensorimotor	Birth to 2 years	Knowledge is based on sensory input and motor skills. Major accomplishment is development of mental representation.
Preoperational	2 to 6 years	Use of symbols advances significantly, moving towards understanding of words and numbers to represent the world. Very egocentric and unable to see other people's point of view.
Concrete Operational	7 to 11 years	Child develops understanding of logical operations and reversibility of operations, but application exists only for information in the here and now.
Formal Operational	Adolescence and beyond	Abstract thought and speculation of hypothetical situations develops, in addition to the ability to reason deductively.

Fig. 12 Piaget's four stages of cognitive development occur in a universal order, though not necessarily at the ages indicated.

stages, but the ages that they occur can vary dramatically based on children's individual differences.

To understand this differentiation, it is important to think about the process of development from a physical perspective as an example. In terms of physical stature, children universally grow taller over time. They do not grow and then shrink and then grow again repeatedly until they reach their final height. Rather, while growth progression varies greatly with each individual child, the process is continuous with children retaining the growth of earlier stages. This analogy is applied to what is believed about Piaget's stage theory – while cognitive growth can occur at different ages, the growth that does occur happens in an orderly sequence that is immutable and subsumes previous growth in earlier stages.

Piaget's evaluations of the unalterable nature of the sequence of stages came mostly through the study of his own three children. Using his semi-structured interview technique, he was able to gain insight into a child's thinking processes by testing their understanding via a multitude of tasks. Rather than a highly structured and standardized process, like the intelligence test that Piaget had administered in Alfred Binet's laboratory in Paris, this process allows for deeper insight into a detailed understanding of the cognitive stage of the child (albeit in a very non-standardized way, which has led many people to question the reliability and validity of these measurement techniques).

This interview technique became synonymous with Piaget and has yielded an outstanding body of research that would have been undiscovered using more formal, standardized techniques. In essence, this method asks a child an initial question that is similar across children under study, but the individual child's answers determine the subsequent question asked by Piaget. By following the child's line of thinking, Piaget assumed he would be able to dive more deeply into understanding the way in which the child was actually processing the information under discussion. He rejected the popular notion that it was important to simply understand the level of intelligence of a child based on a structured standardized intelligence test. Rather, he felt the richest and most important information would unfold through a process of a semi-structured interaction with an adult providing general questions guided by the child's responses.

While his non-quantitative evaluations of his children are certainly detailed and impressive, this insight about the sequential nature of knowledge acquisition remains a difficult concept to evaluate through more empirical investigations. Beyond the studies that Piaget conducted on his own children, other researchers have attempted to determine whether the stages are unalterable or whether they could be hurried, often developing innovative techniques to analyze these central assumptions of Piaget's epistemological theory. To do this, researchers have created carefully proscribed training programs to try to speed up the cognitive development of certain children. The results of such studies have indicated that little or no additional growth can be detected, suggesting that the stages are indeed immutable. Piaget had also determined that while children pass through the stages in the same sequence, the ages at which they move from stage to stage can vary greatly based on individual differences. So, while many children reach the concrete operational stage by age seven, some children reach it earlier and some later based on characteristics of the individual.

Piaget's theory of cognitive development suggests that children move through fairly universal stages that are fundamentally different in quality. These stages are hierarchical, building upon previous stages, but akin to children gaining a continually more accurate perception of the reality of their environment – going from a low-resolution to a high-resolution viewing of the world as they mature. Unlike his contemporary, the Soviet psychologist Lev Vygotsky (1896–1934), who believed that cognitive development was mainly propelled via social interaction, Piaget believed that (individual) action alone propelled children through the stages of development that he described. For Piaget, the active process was an innate mechanism, continually evolving and driven by natural curiosity. While Piaget did provide age ranges for each of the stages of cognitive development, it should be reiterated that the age ranges were an estimate and that variability exists regarding when individual children pass through each of the stages.

5. The Moral Judgement of the Child

Understanding how children learn the difference between right and wrong behaviour was another area of comprehensive study for Piaget. His interests in moral development were primarily focused on how children come to understand three areas of moral reasoning: rules, responsibility, and justice and how these notions evolve over time as children get older.

Just as his study of development within the cognitive domain was unconventional, so was his methodological approach to understanding children's moral reasoning. Piaget felt that observing children playing games together within realistic 'lab-like' settings and querying them during and after the games was the most effective approach to uncover the development of morality in humans. This innovative approach to moral understanding yielded previously unknown ideas regarding the details of children's moral thinking. Piaget's book *The Moral Judgement of the Child* (1932), was a revolutionary look at moral reasoning that was fairly unknown outside of French-speaking countries until the mid-to-late 20th century.

While Piaget is best known for describing the cognitive maturity of the developing child, his constructivist philosophy of cognitive development is mirrored in his theories on moral development. Understanding the ever-decreasing egocentrism that unfolds as a child gets older allows for advancements in understanding morality. Piaget studied the growth of moral reasoning from infancy through to adolescence, believing the interplay between a child's thoughts and actions to be the engine that drives the development of moral reasoning. Generally defined as the process by which children develop their conceptualizations of right or wrong based on laws and cultural norms, moral development is vitally important to understand within the developing child.

Moral Stages

Just as Piaget felt that cognitive development unfolds as a child interacts with his environment, he also believed that moral development occurs in stages and is generally an autonomous process driven by the individual child. While the complexity of cognition unfolds in four discrete stages according to Piaget, he described moral development as only two stages or types of moral reasoning that occur in order: heteronomous and autonomous.

The first stage of moral thinking, heteronomous morality (moral realism), is imposed from the outside whereby we obey the rules of authority. The second stage or type of moral thinking is autonomous morality (moral relativism) which is based on our own rules. It is here that we can see Kant's influence: autonomy allows us to be our own moral judge.

Heteronomous Morality

Piaget believed that children from approximately age five to nine years typically fall into the 'heteronomous morality' category. Characterized by an emphasis on obeying rules and laws set forth by others, children in the heteronomous stage believe that rules and laws cannot be changed; that they are indisputable and absolute. They accept that rules are made by authority figures and that disobeying them will lead to punishment (McLeod, 2015).

Outcome Over Intention

At this stage, if a child sees a misbehaviour, then the event is seen as 'bad', based purely on observation. There is no nuance for the intention of the action. To understand a child's stage of moral development, Piaget told stories that would try to uncover the moral reasoning of the child. Here is an example:

> *'There was once a little girl who was called Marie. She wanted to give her mother a nice surprise and cut out a piece of sewing for her, but she didn't know how to use scissors properly and cut a big hole in her dress.*
>
> *A little girl called Margaret went and took her mother's scissors one day when her mother was out. She played with them for a bit. Then, as she didn't know how to use them properly, she made a little hole in her dress.'*
> (Piaget, 1932)

Piaget would then ask the child listening to the story, 'Who is naughtier?' Younger children typically judge the naughtiness in terms of the outcome of the behaviour rather than the motive or intention of the behaviour, therefore they were more likely to suggest that Marie is naughtier as she cut a 'big' hole in the dress, whereas Margaret cut a 'small' hole.

Punishment in Proportion

Younger children also feel that punishment should be in proportion to the extent of the misbehaviour or lie told. For example, if one child says they saw a mouse the size of a hippopotamus and another says they saw a mouse the size of a dog, the first child would be seen as naughtier as their lie was bigger (more exaggerated) and therefore younger children would conclude that they should receive a harsher punishment. The younger child would also expect the punishment to be carried out immediately following the bad behaviour. This notion of imminent justice pervades the responses from younger children and follows along the lines of the 'eye for an eye' retribution ideal from the Old Testament. These younger children also feel that bad behaviour is always met with punishment no matter the person or situation.

Tattle-Tailing

Another characteristic of this concept of retribution, punishment, and unilateral consequences for any misdeed, is that younger children are also much more likely to tell on others for bad behaviour. This 'tattle-tailing' stems from their belief that it is always their obligation to let adults know of wrongdoings.

Autonomous Morality

The more advanced stage of moral reasoning, 'autonomous morality', is morality based on our own rules and understanding of the moral workings of society. For Piaget, by about 9 or 10 years of age (although there is variability) moral understanding of the world undergoes a radical conversion to allow a more accurate perception of the viewpoints of others when evaluating moral issues. Children are now able to put themselves in 'someone else's shoes'. It is at this point that children's thinking starts to resemble adults and their understanding of the nature of rules and the concept of justice itself becomes significantly more advanced. For example, they understand that, in real life, the concept of justice is more complicated and that sometimes innocent people are found guilty and guilty people get away with misdeeds. Prior to this point, Piaget theorized that younger children believe in a divine-like arbiter of rules but once they have reached the autonomous morality stage, they begin to understand that people make rules and that the rules are changeable.

Good Intentions

Children also begin to accept there is not always an absolute right or wrong and that, when judging the severity of a wrongdoing, the most important aspect to consider is the intentions rather than the outcomes or extent of the misbehaviour or lie. In the example above where Marie and Margaret both cut a hole in their mother's dress, children in the more advanced stage of moral development would say that Margaret was the naughtier child as Marie wanted to give her mother a nice surprise, despite the unfortunate outcome. They would therefore recognize that Marie had good intentions behind her actions. Here we see a large shift in the conceptualization of morality within the developing child. This new understanding of the importance of intention dramatically alters their views of right and wrong and the doling out of punishment for those who break rules.

Fair Play

Older children recognize that the concept of fairness is of primary importance within game play. The more sophisticated understanding of the nature of rules helps older children to recognize that sometimes rules need to be altered depending on circumstances and they are able to apply reason to games and conflicts. This newfound moral relativism, according to Piaget, occurs due to a cognitive reorganization as most children at this stage are beginning to overcome their deeply egocentric thinking and are able to take on perspectives that differ to their own more easily.

Telling Lies

In terms of lying, older children begin to recognize that sometimes lies are necessary. The concept of 'little white lies' to protect the feelings of others is now more widely understood as a positive act. In addition, a greater understanding of the problems with lying also develops. Younger children most often assume lying is wrong because you get punished by adults. Older children recognize that lying undermines trust and can have an effect on relationships.

Punishment

Piaget also found that children over the ages of 9 or 10 are likely to have a more nuanced understanding of punishment. Rather than a revengeful attitude towards those who misbehave or lie, older children tend to desire the offender to understand why they were wrong and to make amends for it. For example, if a person destroys property, older children would likely feel that part of the punishment and restitution would be for the offender to repair the damage.

Methods of Investigating Moral Reasoning

One of the most fascinating facets of Piaget's study of moral reasoning is the methods he used to uncover how children develop morality. In his book, *The Moral Judgement of the Child* (1932), Piaget recounts how he spent endless hours watching boys playing the game of marbles which he conceived to be the ideal game to reveal how children develop morality principles. He explains:

> *'[...] the rules of the game of marbles are handed down, just like so-called moral realities. [...] The little boys who are beginning to play are gradually trained by the older ones in respect for the law; and in any case they aspire from their hearts to the virtue, supremely characteristic of human dignity, which consists in making a correct use of the customary practices of a game. As to the older ones, it is in their power to alter the rules. If this is not "morality", then where does morality begin?'* (Piaget, 1932)

Beyond simple unobtrusive observation, Piaget's favoured technique was feigned naivety. When watching the children play the games, he would pretend to be ignorant of the rules and ask children to explain them. This technique proved to be masterful as he was able to evaluate how the children understood the rules and how well children across age ranges followed the rules of the game. In his quest to understand the morally developing child, Piaget became fascinated regarding what children think in terms of the rules themselves.

A second technique that Piaget would use to understand the moral compass of a particular child was to relate a short story (like that mentioned earlier with Marie and Margaret) or a scenario that describes a child (or adult) carrying out some form of misbehaviour. The example below is one such 'scenario':

'Q: Is one of the boys [who broke the teacups] naughtier than the other?

A: The first is because he knocked over twelve cups.

Q If you were the daddy, which one would you punish the most?

A: The one who broke twelve cups.

Q: Why did he break them?

A: The door shut too hard and knocked them. He didn't do it on purpose.

Q: And why did the other boy break a cup?

A: He wanted to get the jam. He moved too far. The cup got broken.

Q: Why did he want to get the jam?

A: Because he was all alone. Because his mother wasn't there.

Q: Have you got a little brother?

A: No, a little sister.

Q: Well, if it was you who had broken the twelve cups when you went into the room and your little sister who had broken one cup when she was trying to get the jam, which of you would be punished more severely?

A. Me, because I broke more than one cup.' (Piaget, 1932)

From this dialogue, it is obvious that the child who broke 12 cups didn't do it on purpose but that, due to the severity of the outcome (12 broken cups), the little boy being questioned felt the punishment should be more severe than for the boy who only broke one cup. Adults and children who have reached moral autonomy would of course understand that punishment is not based on the outcome of the wrongdoing but rather, on the intention.

Criticisms of Piaget's Methodology

As with other aspects of Piaget's theory of the developing child, there are significant criticisms about his approach to understanding moral development. Foremost, the critiques are aimed at his methodology. Piaget's procedures for understanding moral development are based almost exclusively on observations. While providing detailed information regarding how children at different ages respond to a variety of morally stimulating situations, the procedures are lacking in scientific rigour. He did not conduct sophisticated experiments or highly structured testing protocols, so significant subjectivity was present within the administration and interpretation of his studies. The lack of controlled experimental designs with large samples of children made it difficult to determine it Piaget's findings are generalizable to children across cultures.

Another criticism is that Piaget spent more time focused on boys than girls. While not uncommon for the time, this minimizing of the female perspective is seen as a significant detractor from the application of his ideas. One such critique came from psychologist Carol Gilligan (b. 1936) who criticized Piaget – and other male psychologists – of holding negative views of feminine morality by not spending equal time studying both sexes. In her book *In a Different Voice* (1982), Gilligan develops her own theory that men and women have different conceptions of moral understanding; the male morality being based on rules and abstract principles of justice, while the female morality is based on care and compassion.

Indeed, one need only read earlier literature to know that firstly, in Piaget's time most psychologists were men, and secondly, that the language used was by and large sexist, so Gilligan's study is much needed. But one could argue in Piaget's favour that he spent years studying his daughters (as well as his son), so much of his work would have included both boys and girls. In addition, his focus on the game of marbles in *The Moral Judgement of the Child* was down to the way its rules fulfilled all the defining conditions of a moral system, rather than Piaget specifically choosing to study boys over girls. As Piaget says: 'We did not succeed in finding a single collective game played by girls in which there were as many rules and, above all, as fine and consistent an organization and codification of these rules as in the game of marbles.' (1932)

Instead, Piaget chose the game of 'Marelle' (or 'hopscotch' in English) 'which consists in hopping on one leg and kicking a stone through various sections drawn on the ground', although the game 'never presents the splendid codification and complicated jurisprudence of the game of marbles'. Piaget goes on, 'As to the game of marbles itself, the few little girls who take any interest in it seem more concerned with achieving dexterity at the game than with the legal structure of this social institution' (Piaget, 1932). Finally Piaget settled on studying girls playing a form of hide-and-seek:

> *'As the game is simple and only girls are questioned, the conditions before us are as different as possible from the boys' game of marbles. Such analogies as do eventually appear will therefore be all the more valuable.'* (1932)

The conclusions that Piaget drew from his study of girls were that they were less keen to conform than boys and 'more tolerant and more easily reconciled to innovations'. Despite this, however, he surmises that,

> *'[...] in spite of these differences in structure of the game and, apparently, in the players' mentality [girls differing from boys], we find the same process at work as in the evolution of the game of marbles: first a mystical respect for the law, which is conceived as untouchable and of transcendental origin, then a co-operation that liberates the individuals from their practical egocentrism and introduces a new and more immanent conception of rules.'* (1932)

As we can see, Piaget did show concern with gaining a balanced view of both male and female child development but perhaps, in much the way that his methodology lacked in scientific rigour, the breadth of his observations could have gone further.

6. Application of Piaget's Theories

For Piaget, '[t]he goal of education is to create men and women who are capable of doing new things' (Piaget quoted in Benson et al., 2012). Piaget's words on what constitutes the goal of educating children were transformative to the educational world. While not universally adopted, many educational institutions spanning the globe altered the way they approached teaching and learning based on the work of Jean Piaget. Even to this day, Piaget's ideas pervade the educational domain to such an extent that they have become common knowledge. Educators fundamentally understand that teaching should encompass more than the passive transmission of information; children must be participants in their own learning. Robert Slavin (2006), a foremost developmental psychologist of the 21st century has described four main teaching implications (adapted below) that can be drawn from the work of Piaget.

1. The process of how children come to answers is as important as the final product. Teachers should place emphasis on more than just final answers generated and ensure that students understand the steps they took to come to their final answers.

2. The focus in the classroom should be on active rather than passive learning. Piaget felt that self-initiated, self-directed learning was the key to true knowledge acquisition and that children must be actively involved in their learning. Children are encouraged to discover via unprompted interaction with their environment.

3. De-emphasis of teacher practices that make children's thinking akin to adult thinking and encourages acceleration beyond the level of which a child may be ready. Piaget often spoke of the American question: How can I move my child faster through the stages of cognitive development? Piaget felt it was inappropriate to speed up instruction to accelerate the learning of students who were not at the developmentally appropriate level.

4. Understanding of wide-spread individual differences in developmental progress. Because Piaget felt the ages at which students passed thorough the stage of cognitive development varied greatly, he emphasized the need for teachers to focus on individualizing instruction and creating small groups rather than focusing on class-wide learning activities.

In the United States and throughout Europe in the 1970s and 80s, many schools evolved to incorporate a child-centred model as the primary focus of education. No longer were kids to be lined up row by row at formal desks waiting for teachers to impart bits and pieces of disconnected knowledge. Piaget's method encourages the grouping of students together at tables and encourages discovery of knowledge with a teacher acting as a guide on the side rather than a sage on the stage. Teachers are encouraged to engage students to think and come up with innovative solutions, using divergent skills to solve problems. The Piagetian model suggests that educators focus on creating educational environments that inspire people to create and invent rather than regurgitate facts. Conformity and guidelines for learning are actively discouraged, focusing instead on sparking the imaginations of the students. Piaget felt so strongly that the natural unfolding of learning is highly active and exploratory from the beginning stages of infancy onward, that he believed schools should be set up as institutions that foster those biological drives, leading to the most effective learning outcomes.

Beyond the focus on innovation, discovery, and creativity, Piaget strongly encouraged educators to be aware of the 'readiness' of individual students. He felt that it was detrimental to push students beyond what they were ready to learn. He believed that teachers should develop tasks that match the individual student's cognitive level and capabilities and that students should have ample opportunities to interact with each other and ideally teach other students as well. Piaget felt that the active discussions with peers would deepen and consolidate knowledge.

Pervading all of the concepts of Piagetian genetic epistemology is the presupposition that all learning is an active personal process. Unlike the rigid, passive educational settings that dominated formal places of learning in the early part of the 20th century, Piaget broke through old ideas to help educators across the world to see that children are self-directed learners who use their sensory capacities to interact with the world.

Motivation in Schools

Motivation is of primary focus for educators of all stripes. Within behavioural psychology, which had a dominating influence on the educational systems in the United States and to a lesser extent Europe throughout much of the early and mid-20th century, the mechanism for motivation is reinforcement. Motivation for task completion is seen as entirely external to the child who is a passive recipient of the reinforcement, or in some cases punishment. Piaget's thoughts on motivation were a significant departure from the behavioural perspective and more in line with what current research in the field of motivation supports: high quality intrinsic motivation fostered through self-directed learning with minimal effects of reinforcements. Piaget felt that children were motivated due to the occurrence of disequilibration. The cognitive conflicts that arise in an educational environment should be used by educators to encourage children to independently determine how to reduce the conflict through actively assimilating or accommodating their schemas (see Chapter 3).

For Piaget, the natural enthusiasm for learning should be fostered, not diminished by the implementation of punishments and reinforcers. Knowledge construction, he believed, is akin to being a passionate detective. As students begin to learn and explore their environment, they will want to actively pursue answers to the questions they formulate to solve the 'mysteries'. Innate curiosity about the world should be the driver of children's motivation, with teachers using students' interests for enhanced learning:

> *'The traditional school imposes [...] work on the student [...] The new school (constructivist school), on the contrary, appeals to real activity, to spontaneous work based upon personal need and interest.'* (Piaget, 1970a)

Piaget was a proponent of self-directed learning as a way of increasing motivation. When children tell educators what they want to focus on for their learning, they are, according to Piaget, telling the source of their disequilibrium – giving valuable insight into how best to meet their current educational needs.

Piaget's Constructivism

> *'A student who achieves a certain knowledge through free investigation and spontaneous effort will later be able to retain it; he will have acquired a methodology that can serve him for the rest of his life.'* (Piaget, 1968)

Making Sense of Mathematics

Piaget believed that, in mathematics, the focus should be on a student's autonomous thinking and the self-construction of individual mathematical concepts. During the mid-to late-20th century, the focus of maths education in most schools was computation and memorization of algorithms, instead of having students uncover the solution via means that made sense to them.

Six constructivist principles of mathematics have been described by followers of the Piagetian methods. The following have been expanded from Wadsworth (2004):

1. Psychological structures (schemas; see Chapter 3) must be developed before numerical questions

are introduced. If children have not acquired the necessary structures for particular mathematical concepts and questions, the problems presented by educators will lack meaning.

2. Psychological structures must be developed before formal symbolism is introduced. Children must have a clear understanding of written numbers prior to attempting to understand the underlying concepts.

3. Automatized knowledge (memorization) should not be stressed before implicit logic (grasping the underlying concept). Students should be primarily encouraged to gain theoretical understanding.

4. Children must have the opportunity to invent (construct) mathematical relations rather than simply confront ready-made adult thought. Students must have an opportunity to explore and construct mathematical concepts.

5. Teachers must understand the nature of children's mistakes. Instead of punitive measures for incorrect answers, educators should see errors as opportunities for insight into a student's thinking.

6. The correct atmosphere for thinking must be established. Create an active rather than a passive learning environment in which children are encouraged to think deeply about mathematical concepts rather than sitting as passive vessels of knowledge transfer.

Reading and Writing

Many authors have taken time to evaluate methodologies for teaching reading through a Piagetian lens (Elkind, 1981; Devries and Kohlberg, 1987; Wadsworth, 1978). Their extensive evaluations of Piagetian concepts have been summarized into five principles. These ideas have been used by constructivist educators to enhance learning in the domains of reading and writing.

1. Teaching children to read should be connected with all aspects of written language so should not be isolated from teaching spelling and writing. All three subjects should be taught together.

2. Understanding that graphic symbols (written words) represent things is the foundation of reading instruction. Understanding this fundamental principle is the basic building block of learning to read.

3. There is a difference between learning to read and reading. Learning to decode the written language is a fundamentally different skill than reading for understanding. Active effort to decode the written language must be employed by students.

4. Reading content should be meaningful to the child. There must be a certain level of prerequisite knowledge for children to make sense of the books they are reading.

5. Motivation to read is imperative and interest in the material is a strong determinant of readiness to learn to read.

When it comes to reading instruction, of particular importance is the debate between whole language and phonics instruction that has raged among educators of younger children for several decades. While, in general, the whole language approach (an educational philosophy focused on recognizing whole words rather than aiming to always sound out words phonetically) more closely aligns with Piagetian constructivism, many programs claiming to be whole language are not consistent with constructivism. This could account for some of the ineffectiveness in such programs. Current research in the area of reading suggests that for children struggling to learn to read, a more structured phonetic approach is necessary to achieve successful decoding of written words (Hannford, 2020).

Summary of a Piagetian Education

Piaget's thoughts on applying the fundamentals of genetic epistemology to the field of education can be summed up by the following quote: 'Play is the answer to the question, "How does anything new come about?"' Piaget's thoughts about the transmission of knowledge from teacher to student were – and still are – radical compared to the typical classroom structure within the majority of schools across the world:

> *'It is obvious that the teacher as organizer remains indispensable in order to create the situations and construct the initial devices which present useful problems to the child. Secondly, he is needed to provide counterexamples that compel reflections and reconsiderations of overhasty solutions. What is desired is that the teacher cease being a lecturer satisfied with*

> *transmitting ready-made solutions; his role should be that of a mentor stimulating initiative and research.'* (Piaget, 1973)

Piagetian Ideas and Contemporary Neuroscience

While Piaget died before modern neuroscience took hold, in 2017 researchers Scott Bolton and John Hattie explored his theories in the context of findings from the field of neuroscience. Specifically, they were interested in evaluating whether anatomical and physiological brain development corresponds to Piaget's stage theory of development. Their review provides support for the notion that the development of the human brain increases in complexity in stages that are analogous to Piaget's four stages – a rather surprising finding that revives some of the constructivist ideas that have been eclipsed by newer cognitive information processing models. This is an interesting field of study that will need to be critically evaluated as the technologies progress in the field of neuroscience to allow for a better examination of the correspondences between the structural aspects of Piaget's stages.

Criticisms of Piagetian Methods

Despite the widespread adoption of Piagetian methods, through the 1970s and 80s especially, his ideas were met with fierce criticism with the accuracy of his stances being repeatedly questioned. One of the main criticisms is with the foundational precept of cognitive development occurring in discrete stages. Klahr and MacWhinney (1998) and others provide evidence that cognitive development is much more continuous than stage-like. In addition, depending on the formulation of the tasks, later researchers trying to replicate Piaget's findings found discrepancies (Siegler, 1998). During object permanence and hypothesis testing, they discovered that, depending on the way the task was designed or worded, children much younger than anticipated could successfully complete the tasks presented. There are also continuing concerns about whether the results of Piaget's studies were largely culturally influenced instead of being universal notions applicable to humans worldwide (Weitan,1992). Beyond the accusations that Piaget's findings may be only accurate for individuals growing up in the Western world, his beliefs about the final stage of development were considered to be overly optimistic in general. His research was highly skewed towards an educated population and therefore not applicable to the greater society at large (Weitan,1992).

Additional significant criticism was aimed at Piaget's original suppositions about cognitive development over-estimating the abilities of adolescents and under-estimating the abilities of infants. While Piaget gave general age ranges for his four stages, many educators have taken an absolutist perspective to these and indicated that individual differences in children make the stage model inadequate as a way to conceptualize cognitive development in a universal way. For example, highly intellectually gifted children (like Piaget himself) tend to move much more quickly through the stages than anticipated by the model proposed by Piaget. In addition, others have argued that his focus on the need for an action-oriented approach leaves out children without the capacity for such physical action who are still capable of normal cognitive development.

While criticism of his ideas are plentiful, most educational scholars admit it is imperative for a child to be engaged and actively involved in their learning for optimal cognitive development. Just like many other philosophies that are applied broadly across institutions, Piaget's ideas were and are misinterpreted and employed in a very narrow way, focusing only on the active process and neglecting that some educational skills (such as reading decoding) may need to be taught more directly, especially for some individuals.

Despite these criticisms, Piaget continues to remain significant into the 21st century, albeit less so than in the latter part of the 20th century. His contribution lives on throughout many educational and psychological fields and is still readily applied to our overall understanding of children. In fact, his ideas fundamentally changed the way children are perceived on the most essential level. No longer do adults (and government entities) view children as miniature adults. Piaget helped to expose that children are different in kind (qualitative difference in understanding of the world) rather than just different in amount (quantitative difference in how much knowledge they have acquired).

Conclusion

'Sigmund Freud discovered the unconscious, it is said, and Piaget discovered the conscious.' (Hall in Piaget, 1970)

Over a 70-year span, Jean Piaget has given the world more than 50 books and monographs, in addition to over 500 journal articles. Explaining his remarkable – yet simple – ideas about the origin and growth of knowledge within humans, the impact of his ideas is beyond measure. His intellectual reach spans the globe and his ideas have permeated well into the 21st century. After an initial delay due to language barriers, Piaget's ideas have saturated the educational realm and continue to be used decades after his passing, making him one of the most cited authors in the field of child psychology (Tryphon & Bond, 1998).

Piaget evaluated challenging philosophical questions about the study of reality and turned them into more manageable investigations of the development of knowledge acquisition. Questions such as, 'What is reality?' were transformed into more applicable queries such as, 'How do humans acquire knowledge?' This move from the ontological to epistemological is a defining feature of how Piaget's study of psychological development profoundly moved important questions closer to a more measurable theoretical framework than had been studied before.

Unlike his contemporaries, Piaget was not interested in comparing the quantitative (objective) growth of children's intellectual abilities, but rather understanding the complexities of the qualitative (subjective) changes that happen during cognitive development. His inadvertent discovery in Alfred Binet's lab in 1919 – his realization that the acquisition of knowledge was more than just quantitative increases – fundamentally changed the way society views children. No longer were they seen (inappropriately) as smaller versions of adults; Piaget's research fuelled the push to treat children as developing organisms that need to be understood based on their cognitive understanding of the world. His theory that the way children view their environment is a low level of resolution compared to the fully formed adult view has guided our understanding of children and likely led to countless protections of childhood that continue into the 21st century.

Of practical significance, Piaget's legacy is long-lasting with his ideas having transformed the educational systems in Europe and the United States. In 1955, Nathan Isaac (1895–1966), a British educational psychologist and a strong advocate for primary school science education, published *Some Aspects of Piaget's Work*. This influential interpretation of Piaget's theories led to three teacher guides being produced in the UK by the Nuffield Junior Science Project (1963–67), as well as shaping the approach of the Oxford Primary Science Project in 1964. According to C.K. Mackay in his paper 'Piaget and education: a positive comment' (1983), Piaget's principles were the basis for science curriculums in the English-speaking parts of the world, namely 'Science 5–13' in the UK, 'Australian Science Education Project' in Australia, and 'Science Curriculum Improvement Study' in the United States (Mackay, 1983). In the 1970s, when traditional education appeared to be failing in certain parts of the UK, 'Piaget [showed] how to solve this problem—by allowing the teachers more initiative, more freedom and a better grounding in child psychology and research' (Pulaski quoted in Kohler, 2008). In sum, Piaget has inspired educators to create more child-centred methods which focus on high-quality engagement and individualization and are based on the needs of each child.

Beyond the prominent role of active learning, Piaget believed the fundamental purpose of education was to encourage and inspire children and adults to create and innovate. He was adamantly opposed to forced conformism within educational systems or any practice that would stifle the natural curiosity and imagination that comes with childhood. In addition, instead of viewing intelligence as a singular construct represented by a quantitative number, Piaget said this about intelligent behaviour: 'Intelligence is what you use when you don't know what to do.' (Piaget,1926).

Despite his copious achievements and discoveries in cognitive development, continued criticisms have been aimed at Piaget in regard to the methodologies he employed throughout his academic career. While these criticisms are valid based on standard scientific procedures, the powerful nature of the methods Piaget used should not be underestimated. Although they are not comparable to the stringent statistical analyses that now dominate the field of psychology, the movement of conceptualizing complex questions and transforming them into theoretically measurable frameworks was groundbreaking within the study of child development in the 20th century. In addition, Piaget's highly developed clinical interviewing technique was pioneering and became a model for various subsets of psychology.

Piaget's legacy is multifaceted, but his major achievement was his audacity and fortitude in moving the field of psychology forward to delve deeply into understanding human knowledge acquisition beyond the simplistic dichotomy of nature versus nurture. Furthermore, he went beyond the philosophical foundations of Kantian philosophy to create an applicable model for educators to improve the learning outcomes for children. His understanding of the development of knowledge as the result of a complex interaction between the biological and environmental seems obvious to most people in the 21st century. However, we cannot underestimate how Piaget's notions moved our understanding of human development to its current sphere. He was able to look beyond behaviourism and, to a lesser extent, psychoanalysis, both of which dominated the American and European psychological landscapes pre-1950. Not only that but, as one of the founders of cognitive psychology, Piaget opened up the way for others who were looking for an alternative to behaviourism. Erik Erikson (1902–1994) was one such psychologist who embraced developmental psychology over behaviourism; and Lawrence Kohlberg (1927–1987) wouldn't have become the eminent psychologist in moral development that he did had it not been for Piaget.

Piaget's work on religion was also of great influence, with various scholars applying his cognitive stages to children's understanding of religious concepts (Elkind, 1961; Kohlberg & Power, 1981; Goldman, 1964). In philosophy, Piaget's theory on rule-governed behaviour influenced the political philosophers, John Rawls (1921–2002) in his *A Theory of Justice* (1971) and Jürgen Habermas (b. 1929) in his works *The Theory of Communicative Action* (1981) and *Moral Consciousness and Communicative Action* (1983). Piaget was also recognized in the world of computer science where 'Seymour Papert and his colleagues at MIT used Piaget's theory in 1967 as a basis for the Logo Programming Language, a subset of LISP, designed as an educational aid for children' (Sebesta, 1996).

By applying his knowledge from a multitude of domains of study – biology, mathematics, logic, philosophy, and of course psychology – Piaget's research could be applied to so many different fields. While his genetic epistemology can be dense and complex, his principle theoretical proposition was, as Albert Einstein put it, 'so simple, only a genius could have thought of it' (quoted in Papert, 1999).

Bibliography

Works by Piaget

Piaget, J. (1926) *The Language and Thought of the Child*, New York: Harcourt, Brace.

Piaget, J. (1928) *The Child's Conception of the World*, London: Routledge and Kegan Paul.

Piaget, J. (1932) *The Moral Judgement of the Child*, London: Kegan, Paul, Trench, Trubner & Co.

Piaget, J. (1952) 'Jean Piaget', In Boring, Ed., Langfield, H., Werner, H., & Yerkes, R. (eds.). *A History of Psychology in Autobiography, IV*, Worcester, MA: Clark University Press.

Piaget, J. & Cook, M. T. (1952) *The Origins of Intelligence in Children*, New York, NY: International University Press.

Piaget, J. & Inhelder, B. (1963) *The Child's Conception of Space* (trans. by F.J. Lagdon and J.L. Lunzer), London: Routledge & Kegan Paul.

Piaget, J., Inhelder, B. & Weaver, H. (1969) *The Psychology of the Child*, New York: Basic Books.

Piaget, J. & Seagrim, G.N. (1969). *The Mechanisms of Perception* (trans. by G.N. Seagrim), New York: Basic Books.

Piaget, J. (1970) 'A Conversation with Jean Piaget and Barbel Inhelder: Interview by Elizabeth Hall', *Psychology Today*, 3.

Piaget, J. (1970a) *Genetic Epistemology* (trans. by E. Duckworth), New York: Columbia University Press.

Piaget, J. (1970b) *Science of Education and the Psychology of the Child*, New York: Viking Press.

Piaget, J. (1972) *Insights and Illusions of Philosophy,* (trans. by Wolfe Mays), London: Routledge & Kegan Paul.

Piaget, J. (1973) *To Understand is to Invent,* New York: Viking Press.

Piaget, J. (1979) *Genetic Epistemology,* New York: Columbia University Press, 1970.

Piaget, J. & Garcia, R. (1983) *Psychogenesis and the History of Science,* (trans. by H. Feider), New York: Columbia University Press.

Other works cited

Beilin, H. (1992) 'Piaget's enduring contribution to developmental psychology', *Developmental Psychology, 28*(2), pp.191–204.

Benson, N., Collin, C., Ginsburg, J., Grand, V., Lazyan, M., Weeks, M. (2012) *The Psychology Book,* London: Dorling Kindersley Ltd.

Bliss, J. (2010) 'Looking Back: Recollections of Jean Piaget', *The Psychologist,* May 2010, Vol. 23, pp.444–447

Bolton, S. & Hattie, J. (2017) 'Cognitive and Brain Development: Executive Function, Piaget, and the Prefrontal Cortex', *Archives of Psychology, 1*(3)

Bringuier, J. C. (1980) *Conversations with Jean Piaget,* University of Chicago Press.

Devries, R. & L. Kohlberg (1987) *Programs of Early Education: The Constructivist View,* New York: Longman.

Distinguished Scientific Contribution Awards: 1969: Citation for Jean Piaget (1970). *American Psychologist,* 25(1), pp.65–79.

Elkind, D. (1961) 'The Child's Conception of his Religious Denomination', *Journal of Genetic Psychology,* 99, pp.209–225.

Elkind, D. (1962) 'Quantity Conceptions in College Students', *The Journal of Social Psychology, 57*(2), pp.459-465.

Elkind, D. (1981) *Stages in the Development of Reading. IN New Directions in Piagetian Theory and Practice*, edited by I. Sigel, D. Brodinsky & R. Golinkoff, Hillsdale, NJ.: Erlbaum.

Fabricius, W. (1983) 'Piaget's Theory of Knowledge: Its Philosophical Context', *Human Development, 26* pp.325–334.

Flavell, J.H. (1985) *Cognitive Development* (2nd Ed.), Englewood Cliffs, NJ: Prentice Hall.

Gale, Cengage Learning (2015) *A Study Guide for Psychologists and Their Theories for Students: Jean Piaget.*

Goldman, R. (1964) *Religious Thinking from Childhood to Adolescence*, London: Routledge & Kegan Paul.

Gruber, H. & J. Voneche, eds. (1977) *The Essential Piaget,* New York: Basic Books.

Hanford, Emily (2020) 'Kids Struggle to Read When Schools Leave Phonics Out', *The Hechinger Report*, 30 Mar. 2020, retrieved February 25, available at www.hechingerreport.org/kids-struggle-to-read-when-schools-leave-phonics-out/

Inhelder, B., Piaget, J. & Parsons, A. (1961) *An Essay on the Construction of Formal Operational Structures*, New York: Basic Books.

Inhelder, B., Piaget, J., Lunzer, E.A. & Papert, D. (1964) *The Early Growth of Logic in the Child: Classification and Seriation*, London: Routledge and Kegan Paul.

Kail, R.V. (1998) *Children and their Development*, Upper Saddle River, NJ: Prentice Hall.

Kitchener, R. (1988) Review, *Zeitschrift Für Allgemeine Wissenschaftstheorie / Journal for General Philosophy of Science, 19*(1), pp.157–165.

Klahr, D. & MacWhinney, B. (1998) 'Information processing', In W. Damon (ed.), *Handbook of Child Psychology; Vol. 2: Cognition Perception, and Language,* Hoboken, NJ: Wiley.

Kohlberg, L. & Power, C. (1981) 'Moral Development, Religious Thinking and the Question of a Seventh Stage', in L. Kohlberg (ed.), *Essays on Moral Development, I: The Philosophy of Moral Development*, San Francisco: Harper & Row.

Lourenço, O. (2012), 'Piaget and Vygotsky: Many resemblances, and a crucial difference', *New Ideas in Psychology, 30*(3), pp.281-295.

Mackay, C.K. (1983) 'Piaget and Education: A Positive comment', in S. Modgil, C. Modgil & G. Brown (eds.), *Jean Piaget, an Interdisciplinary Critique*, London: Routledge & Kegan Paul.

McLeod, S.A. (2015) 'Piaget's theory of moral development', *Simply Psychology*, retrieved 5 January 2021, available at www.simplypsychology.org/piaget-moral.html

New World Encyclopedia (n.d.) Retrieved 29 June, 2020, available at https://www.newworldencyclopedia.org/entry/Jean_Piaget

Papert, S. (1999) 'Child Psychologist Jean Piaget', *Time*, Monday 29 March, 1999.

Sebesta, R.T. (1996) *Concepts of Programming Languages*, Menlo Park: Addison-Wesley.

Siegler, R.S. (1998) *Children's Thinking* (3rd ed.), Upper Saddle River, NJ: Prentice Hall.

Tryphon, A. & Bond, T.G. (2007) *Piaget's Legacy as Reflected in the Handbook of Child Psychology* (this edition 1998).

Tsou, J.Y. (2006) 'Genetic Epistemology and Piaget's Philosophy of Science', *Theory & Psychology, 16*(2), pp.203–224.

Vidal, F. (1997) 'Re-Reading Jean Piaget', *Human Development, Reflecting on the History of Developmental Research*, pp.124–126.

Wadsworth, B.J. (2004) *Piaget's Theory of Cognitive and Affective Development*, Boston, MA: Pearson.

Weiten, W. (1992) *Psychology: Themes and Variations* (2nd edn), California: Brooks/ Cole Publishing Company.

Biography

Jessica Koehler, PhD, is the author of 'Beyond School Walls' at *Psychology Today*, where she focuses on bringing the science of psychology to learning and life. Dr Koehler currently teaches online classes in psychology and is the co-principal investigator of a research project focused on the social, emotional, and behavioural characteristics of gifted learners. She lives in Utah, USA, with her husband, two homeschooled sons, and two dogs.

Acknowledgements

Foremost, thank you to my husband, Chris. His unwavering support, encouragement, and willingness to entertain Alex and Max – while Mom was writing – were considerable contributions to the successful completion of this book! A special thank you to my grandmother, Genevieve Savani, for being a pioneer in psychology and igniting my interest in human behaviour. I am also grateful to my mom, Becky Savani Gilbert, for her willingness to discuss Piaget's ideas from the perspective of a classroom teacher. I also owe a huge debt of gratitude to Alice Bowden for her fantastic editing – always making each section a bit better than I had left it.

Picture Credits:

Opening image: Piaget. Praagnya1830396, CC BY-SA 4.0 <https://creativecommons.org/licenses/by-sa/4.0>, via Wikimedia Commons. **Fig. 1** 'Lake Neuchâtel, Switzerland, where Piaget grew up', Dmst, CC BY-SA 3.0 <https://creativecommons.org/licenses/by-sa/3.0>, via Wikimedia Commons. **Fig. 2** 'Museum of Natural History, Neuchâtel, Switzerland', Chandres, CC BY-SA 3.0 <https://creativecommons.org/licenses/by-sa/3.0>, via Wikimedia Commons. **Fig. 3** 'University of Neuchâtel, Switzerland', Yves André The original uploader was Unine at French Wikipedia., Public domain, via Wikimedia Commons. **Fig. 4** 'Dr. Eugen Bleuler (1857–1939)', Unknown author, Public domain, via Wikimedia Commons. **Fig. 5** 'Alfred Binet (1857–1911)', Unidentified photographer, Public domain, via Wikimedia Commons. **Fig. 6** 'Piaget with Pierre Bovet (front row) in front of the Rousseau Institute, Geneva, 1925', unknown (upload MHM-com 19:19, 24 December 2007 (UTC)), Public domain, via Wikimedia Commons. **Fig. 7** 'Piaget with his wife Valentine (top right) at a conference at the International Bureau of Education in Geneva in 1932', unknown (upload MHM-com 15:54, 6 January 2008 (UTC)), Public domain, via Wikimedia Commons. **Fig. 8** 'Bust of Jean Piaget in Parc des Bastion in Geneva, Switzerland', MHM55, CC BY-SA 4.0 <https://creativecommons.org/licenses/by-sa/4.0>, via Wikimedia Commons. **Fig. 9** 'An example of the taxonomy of mollusks, 1843', Paul Rang, Public domain, via Wikimedia Commons. **Figs. 10–12** Copyright Bowden & Brazil Ltd.

Aristotle
Plato
Michel Foucault
Friedrich Nietzsche
Immanuel Kant
David Hume
Ludwig Wittgenstein
B. F. Skinner
Jean Piaget
Melanie Klein
Stanley Milgram
Karl Marx
Jean-Jacques Rousseau
Olympe de Gouges
Betty Friedan
Erwin Panofsky

Jane Jacobs

Printed in Dunstable, United Kingdom

78725124R00078